Life on
Croucher's Island

Maggie B. Boutilier

GlenMargaret
PUBLISHING

cover design: Brenda Conroy
editing: Richard Rogers
layout: Richard Rogers
maps: Paul McCormick
cover art: Marijka Simons

Glen Margaret Publishing
P.O. Box 3087
Tantallon, Nova Scotia   B3Z 4G9
TEL/FAX 902-823-1198
www.glenmargaret.com

Canadian Cataloguing in Publication Data
National Library of Canada Cataloguing in Publication

Boutilier, Maggie B. (Maggie Beatrice), 1898-1986.
    Life on Croucher's Island / Maggie B. Boutilier.

ISBN 0-920427-62-6

    1. Boutilier, Maggie B. (Maggie Beatrice), 1898-1986.
    2. Lighthouse keepers' wives–Nova Scotia–Croucher's Island–Biography.
    3. Croucher's Island (N.S.)–Biography. I. Title.

VK1140.B68A3 2003   387.1'55'092   C2003-903637-5

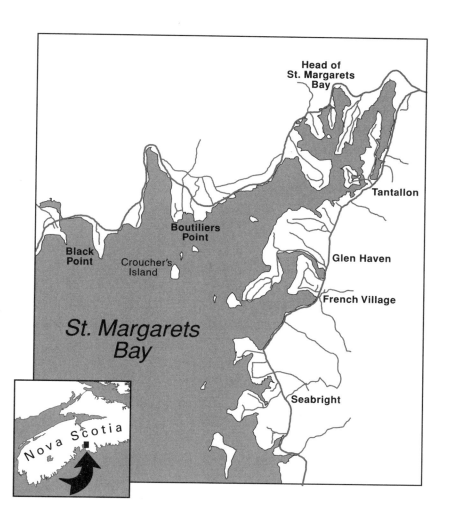

Head of
St. Margarets
Bay

Tantallon

Boutiliers
Point

Black
Point

Croucher's
Island

Glen Haven

French Village

*St. Margarets
Bay*

Nova Scotia

Seabright

Acknowledgement

To my great-nephew, Thane, who spent so many hours reading, rewording and co-ordinating the bits and pieces as I wrote; to Jean who made the copies as they were required; and to my daughter, Joyce, who typed, re-typed, and transported the material to, and from, the two above-mentioned individuals, my deepest appreciation. I couldn't have done it without their help.

Foreword

Please note, as you read, that most of the events in this book have been written with the benefit of memory only as I did not keep a diary. To the best of my knowledge all are chronologically correct. All are actual events.

Yours for happy reading.

Chapter one

There are several versions as to how St. Margaret's Bay was named. My favourite is as follows:

When Samuel de Champlain was exploring the uncharted waters off Canada's Atlantic coast, he sailed into the largest bay in Nova Scotia. Awed by its size and seclusion he was also impressed with its many inlets and the islands, which dotted its placid water. Combined with the beauty of the surrounding hills and the small mountains that were covered with virgin forest, the effect was such that he breathed "Sainte Margarete"! Thus, St. Margaret's Bay.

During the eighteenth century the flow of immigrants to Canada began to increase. Among those who settled around St. Margaret's Bay were the English, French, Swiss and Germans. Gradually, English became the predominant language, Anglican and Lutheran the main religions.

In 1752, with the Huguenot influx, came the Boutiliers from Montebeliard in the province of Etabon, France. Large families were common and most had problems supporting the children. Often a child from a large family would make a prolonged visit to the home of a relative or friend where there were fewer mouths to feed. If a census were taken during this time, the child was often registered, incorrectly, as belonging to the wrong parents. Interesting, but confusing; I do not envy anybody the pleasure of tracing their Boutilier roots.

Settlements and islands were usually named after the person(s) who settled there first; hence, Boutilier's Point, Hubley's Settlement (later changed to Seabright), French Village, Hackett's Cove, and Indian Harbour.

Our island was first granted to a Charles Ingram in the early seventeenth century. It was later purchased by a George Boutilier and became known, locally, as George's Island. The island changed ownership frequently either through bequest or by purchase-and-deed, eventually returning to Boutilier ownership when we purchased it.

One of its many owners was James Croucher, Sr., an educated gentleman whose name the island now bears. Mr. Croucher was a man of some means and would often settle the account of a person in debt in return for a piece of that person's land. It is fantastic the numerous acres of land he acquired in this fashion.

Mr. Croucher owned George's Island at the time the Canadian government purchased a portion of it in February, 1883, for the purpose of erecting a lighthouse. On the charts this was shown as Croucher's Island light, with the result that the island was soon called Croucher's Island even by the local people. That name has endured to the present, and even during our stay there. Though we were Boutiliers and owned the island, our supplies were always sent to Croucher's Island.

James Croucher's grandson, George Croucher, who eventually inherited the island, was the first lightkeeper. His term of service was thirty-eight years. During the last twenty years of his service, he and his family spent their winters on the mainland, while his assistant kept the light. In 1921, when we came into the picture, Frederick Boutilier was acting lightkeeper.

The island consists of approximately twenty acres. It is oval in shape and attached to another island known as Woody island by a sand bar, which is exposed at half ebb tide. There were buildings on both islands as, it seems, they were at one time just one piece of land.

Chapter two

Wentworth Willis Boutilier, born 1890 in Boutilier's Point, moved in his early childhood years to French Village with his parents. He was an academic, intellectual student; an ardent reader and excelled in all types of work. Prior to his military life, Wentie, as he was known, had spent a few summers on coastal vessels. At one point Captain Joshua Dauphinee employed him on his schooner, *Lorne*.

These were small vessels buying from fishermen and supplying merchants along the shore from one small port to another. The sea was the first way of travel. Roads were made later. When the Halifax Southwestern Railway was put through from Halifax to Yarmouth, Nova Scotia, 1904-1905, ships became a secondary business. The young lads in Seabright and French village had to look elsewhere for their seamanship. They, Wentie included, sought employment in the U.S.A. They were sometimes fortunate enough to hire on steam yachts owned by wealthy people, who toured Europe and other parts of the world.

The last voyage Wentie made was in 1910 on the *Gunilda*, which was owned by William Harkness, an oil magnate from New York, U.S.A. They sailed Lake Superior under the command of Captain Alexander Corkum. Captain Corkum requested a pilot onboard during this trip for he was not familiar with these waters, but Mr. Harkness refused. Subsequently the ship went high and dry on an uncharted rock.

Naturally it was a trying time for the owner, guests, commander and crew. Even the tug, *HMS James Whalen*, could not pull the *Gunilda* off the rock. After forty-eight hours, Mr.

The crew of the "Gunilda".

Harkness asked, "Is everybody clear of the ship"? He was told that all had been transported to safety, so he gave the order to cut her loose. She toppled over and sank in minutes without loss of life. The crew held William Harkness in highest esteem for his settlement to them. Regrettably they lost everything they owned–except the clothes they stood in.

An article written in *Chatelaine* some years ago gives an account of the events surrounding the loss of the *Gunilda* but varies slightly from Wentie's on-the-scene version. However, it states that the *Gunilda* is still in perfect condition. A diver has paid Lloyds of England one million dollars for permission to raise her.

Because of his marine experience, Wentie was never afraid in a boat. He seemed to feel content at all times. I wish I could say that for myself, but I can't. There were times when our boat seemed to stand on end and shudder before crashing down on the next sea.

I, Maggie Beatrice Slauenwhite, was born in 1898 at Tantallon, a small village between Head of St. Margaret's Bay and French Village. By grade seven I had the dream of many girls of my age. I wanted to be a nurse, but schooling for the majority of my family ended in, or near, the twelfth year of age. We were then either employed in the home full time or

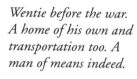

Wentie before the war. A home of his own and transportation too. A man of means indeed.

hired out to other people for a year or two. We were considered high-risk breadwinners.

Born one of thirteen children, I started work at the age of fourteen years. Work consisted of post-natal care, and we earned a dollar a day over a two-week period. I asked for ten dollars a week and was considered "uppity", but I did receive eight.

My early life was happy, being reared in a loving home, until March 1912, when my father was accidentally killed in his own saw mill. Mother mourned her loss to such a degree that our home broke like a bubble. With her four youngest children to support on the earnings of a nineteen-year-old son, Mother was distracted. She would not release us to another member of the family, and there wasn't any government assistance.

Both of our parents had relatives in the U.S.A. who invited Mother and her children to their homes. It took several years of growing for us ere Mother really settled down.

At the age of fifteen I went to the U.S.A. with my mother and worked in Lily Bay House. Lily Bay was on offshoot of

Moosehead Lake, the largest in Maine. The House catered to woodsmen and sportsmen. I worked in the part that catered to woodsmen.

Meanwhile we traveled to and from the U.S.A. a few times. After one of our final trips home from the States, I went to a dance with my cousin. At the time, people danced to music played by violin, accordion, harmonica, jew's-harp, spoons, or anything that beat out a tune, singly or in harmony. On this particular night Wentie was the violinist. Someone spelled him off, and he danced with me; thus started a romance. Six months later on April 13, 1918, we were wed in All Saints Cathedral, Halifax, Nova Scotia. A few days later Wentie joined his regiment and set sail for overseas in World War I.

This is a good place to say that Wentie fought with the 85th Nova Scotia Highlanders. They were in the mopping-up exercises. I often thought this was the reason he required so much quiet, ever alert; wanting to be unseen, yet seeing everything—the ever-constant lookout for a sniper's bullet. He had only two slight wounds; one on the right leg, the other on the left hand. He said, "When marching to the beat of a certain band (he named it, but I don't remember) it was just a steady BOOM, BOOM, BANG. Marching was sheer drudgery, but when the 85th band came up with the bagpipes playing "Sharp Shooter March", that is when they went over the top! Exuberance and new life flowed in their veins. Victory was in their grasp.

There was still much work to be done. Orders required that the terrain and trenches be kept really wet and muddy at all times. As a result, some of the men got trench fever and various other ailments. Wentie's trouble was myalgia legs. The remainder of his military life was spent in hospital. He returned home a stranger—the horrors of war had left their imprint. Even his parents noted the change in his personality. He seemed happiest in the company of the boys he was with while overseas. When a severe, quick thunderstorm would come up you'd see them all scurrying, calling to each other, "It sounds like Over There"!

The cries of pain in conflict with orders to forge ahead,

neither looking left nor right, seeing your boyhood friends and comrades-in-battle falling at your side, is emblazoned in the hearts and minds of all men concerned. To one as reserved and compassionate as Wentie, it seemed to make the memory even deeper. It is little wonder he lived out his days in ill health and melancholy. This explanation may help you understand the change, which took place later in our lives.

He returned home on May 24, 1919. He complained of poor health all the time, took many patented medicines and worked only when his father or brothers were employed on the same job.

Wentie in World War I army uniform. The war left scars, both inside and out, that he carried for the rest of his life.

Chapter three

Our first child, Ethel, arrived on June 10, 1920. Wentie made a fruitful garden alone that summer. He was an excellent woodworking craftsman. Using this talent, he made the baby cradle, crib and high chair. He also made several rocking chairs, some of which he gave to nephews. All were made from pine lumber. An upset soon split the pine chairs, really proving it to be a waste of time and lumber.

Wentie had bought a house in French Village prior to our marriage and lived there with his parents. After we were married, they offered to move out, but I asked them to stay while Wentie was overseas.

In August of 1920 his family put on a "song and dance" about their parents moving out. The answer was "Sell the house to Dad". We could live in two rooms! Although real estate was going up, Dad shouldn't pay more than the purchase price earlier paid by Wentie.

Wentie's mother was a teacup reader–a good one, too. Many people accepted her reading before making a decision. She always saw a big white boat in Wentie's and my cups.

The Soldier's Settlement Board of the Department of Veteran's Affairs was offering farms to returned men. Needless to say, both parties took a "whale of a beating" in the land deal.

Wentie's brother, Cliff, was quite a gambler, or just an ordinary guy looking for a better life. Be that as it may, Cliff saw a farm for sale in Harrietsfield, Halifax County, N.S., in 1920. It was an old farm with a tiny old house and ancient machinery located close to Halifax. Cliff didn't want it, as it seemingly was too far away from Mum and Dad. "What a great place for

Wentie!" He could be a millionaire in a few years, raising a family and all.

Wentie went to see the place, but I didn't accompany him. On his way to Harrietsfield to see the farm he met a man, from whom he stopped to inquire directions. He wanted to know if he was near the Marriot farm. Lo and behold, it was the man who had the farm for sale. Wentie recognized him as Sgt. Golightly, an Army instructor, under whom he had served overseas in World War I. What a reunion!

Mr. Golightly was a Canadian who had married an English "war bride". She didn't have any knowledge of country living, so he took his wife and sons to Toronto, while Wentie was to take his wife and two daughters to an island.

With Cliff's coaching, Wentie bought the farm. He wouldn't move there, because I was pregnant with our second child. Should the truth be known, I think that he was like Cliff–it was too far from the home folks. Our second child, Geraldine, was born August 24, 1921, at my mother's house in Tantallon.

In 1922 tenders were issued for a new keeper of the lighthouse with preference given to a World War One veteran. When Wentie told me he was going to apply for the job, I said, "I do not want to go there for twenty years". He replied, "You don't have to. We will try it for a year. If you don't like it, then we will quit."

He applied. He was working for a lumber company at Bayside, Halifax County, Nova Scotia, when his appointment came through several months later. After a few days of business deals for Wentie, and a little packing for me, we were on our way.

The lighthouse had a full basement, walled with beautifully hand-cut stone slabs, approximately two feet long by one foot wide and possibly ten inches thick. There were three windows in the wall, and each had three light sections.

A large cement cistern was built in the northwest corner to catch rainwater from the sloping roof. The main room began with a slope directly from the sills. The kitchen was smaller

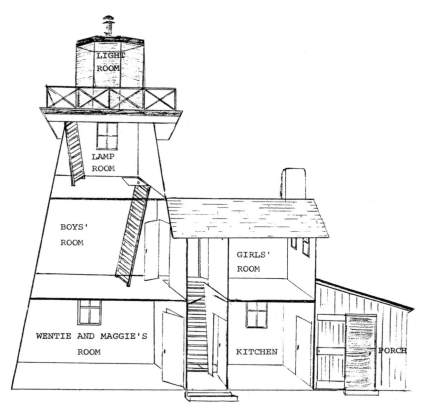

and rose two-and-one-half feet before the slope began. All doors opened from outside on the eastern side of the building, one from the kitchen and one from the wood shed. On the first level, the windows faced east and west. On the second level the windows faced north and south. On the third level, again east and west, and on the fourth level they were all around in an octagon shape as this was the light room.

As well as the cistern located under the lighthouse, there was a well on the island. Water from the cistern was used for washing, scrubbing, and cleaning; while the well water was used for drinking and cooking.

The stairs were inside the front door and sloped steeply, with steps similar to those found in a sailing vessel. Behind those stairs was a small pantry. In front of the pantry door was a heavy trap-hatch, the only entrance to the cellar.

Wentie put a handrail up those stairs and a guardrail around

the hatchway to the second floor. Turn right, and you were in quite a nice bedroom. To the left was a tiny bedroom, with another open flight of stairs and a heavy hatch to lift.

The third floor brought us into a very small room with two large windows, a locker, a stairway and the heaviest iron hatch of them all. This room was used strictly for the cleaning of the lamps. The lamps were made of brass. Each one held two quarts of kerosene oil and barely served through the longest night. Each lamp had only one burner with two wicks. Known as a duplex light, it was guaranteed visible for twelve miles. The fishermen said it was good for fifteen miles and called it their "guiding light".

All brass had to be polished regularly; therefore, the lamp room contained cleaning equipment, including bags of sand in case of fire. No oil was allowed in this room except for immediate service, with one exception. The second lamp had to always be kept in readiness for emergencies.

The fourth floor was made entirely of glass and heavy iron. The walls were octagonal with one panel, which opened for a crawl out door, and was used by the lightkeeper only, to go out on the wooden catwalk if needed. It was very convenient at painting time.

These panels were about three feet high with troughs in the top of them. There was a sheet of plate glass, thirty inches by thirty-six inches, above each panel. Each sheet was surrounded by an iron sash with four heavy hooks above each glass. The hooks held white canvas blinds, which were rolled up by hand at sunset and let down at sunrise. The purpose of the blinds was to protect the prisms and magnifying glass from the sun. The magnifying glass was like an oversized bucket securely fastened on an iron structure, bringing it to a height of about five-and-a-half feet. The lighted lamp had to be lowered into it each evening and taken out each morning. Over all of this was a dome ceiling. The light was stationary.

The troughs were to catch the rain, which often beat in around the windows. Heavy frosts were even worse than rain, freezing by night and thawing by day. Wentie made hooks, which held cans to catch the water. It helped to catch the overflow and one didn't get cold hands while mopping up the wet floor. We still had to carry down buckets of water, night and day, depending on the weather.

I will always remember our first night there! We had taken the baby's cradle and Ethel's crib. Geraldine was not yet a year old; Ethel was twenty-six months.

We slept on an old sack stuffed with straw upon the floor. Our little alarm clock stood on a box beside the bed. It rattled along saying, "Go to sleep, go to sleep". The big old eight-day clock hung on the kitchen wall and it said, "take your time, take your time", while the children breathed deeply and Wentie snored in deep slumber beside me. The moon shone on the placid water while the undercurrent roared like thunder on the shore, driving the rocks high, taking smaller rocks out with it as it receded, sounding like a gasping person struggling for his breath.

It was a beautiful day, but during the night a thick fog settled down over all. Wentie couldn't leave the island and no one came. We had food for only a few days. What a funny feeling; I couldn't even go next door to converse or ask to borrow what I may need, and I couldn't even send to the store to buy what we didn't have on hand.

On Friday Wentie got up, put out the light, left a note for me saying he'd get breakfast ashore and come home as soon as he could. He would bring our stove with him. A person could cook on top of the lighthouse stove, but not bake. The firebox was worn out.

Meanwhile our arrival on the island was early enough to enjoy luscious raspberries, blackberries and tiny little red foxberries. I made delicious jams and jellies from the first two. From the later, which kept well in cold water and could be bailed out, cooked and sweetened at any time, I made delicious dumplings and pies. One of the rules in our Government regulations was that at no time should the island be left unattended. That meant Wentie was free to come and go at will, weather permitting, while I stayed on the job.

We were on the island approximately one month when wanderlust struck me. The day was sunny. At ebb tide I took Dean and a pail on one arm and Ethel by the hand, and ventured forth to Woody island, a nearby island that was home to the greatest flock of hummingbirds that I have ever seen at one time. I put the children on the sand and gave them clamshells for shovels. They played happily, while I picked berries. I kept an eye to the children and the tide, as I greedily picked berries. I wanted to finish picking, as there weren't enough berries to warrant another trip to the island. We stayed a little too long. I took the berries and Dean across the bar. Ethel toddled after us, but would not step into the water, which was rising on the bar. Approximately sixteen or twenty feet of water, only a few inches deep, separated us, but the tiny child stood there holding up her little dress, screaming "Oh Mother, don't leave me here to drown"! I can see it as vividly now as if it were yesterday.

Our first pay-cheque was only forty-seven dollars, which sorely disappointed Wentie. But I had a few hens, so he took some of the money and bought materials to build a small hen house. He was a quiet, ardent worker and was capable of doing most things in a calm environment. Noise disturbed him.

In September, when the second cheque came, his father said, "Wentie, get your food supplies in now".

We bought: a quarter of beef – 148 lbs.
a bag of sugar – 100 lbs.
5 bags of flour – 500 lbs.
a bucket of lard – 20 lbs.
1 case Carnation milk – 48 tins

The beef kept well in the boathouse until May. Our first snowfall had arrived on October 22nd.

In the spring of 1922 one of Wentie's brothers, who lived a mile distant, said that if I would cut potato seed and hire someone to lay them, he'd plow in a patch for me. I accepted his offer and paid a seventy-year-old lady to seed them for me.

After we got some things to keep house with and some

food to eat, the island was beautiful. Our contentment was like the Garden of Eden. So I wrote:

'Twas the 15th day of August
Year 1922
The sun rose high in the Heavens
The water a calm, deep blue
We got into our little boat
And slowly paddled our way
To tend an island lighthouse
Out in St. Margaret's Bay

We landed on the island
Among the fishing crew
Of half a dozen men or more
And only one I knew
Confidently, and with pride
We climbed the stairs that night
To guide the ships from danger
By the beacon of our light

Our friends they came to see us
Likewise strangers unknown
Ere we scarcely realized
The winter had fully flown.

What a winter that was!

Our October cheque was used to buy food for the hens. Cabbage, turnips and carrots were bought from the schooners for household use. These vegetables were raised on the well-populated Ironbound and Tancook Islands, which are situated far out in the Atlantic Ocean. The cabbage was used to make sauerkraut. Wentie made almost a barrel full.

Our clothes and many other purchases were done through the mail order catalogues. We spent many hours shopping ere we finally settled on a purchase.

In October Wentie said, "I'm going to get the things for Christmas. I won't have the children disappointed. You don't know what the weather will be like next month". So Wentie shopped. He bought tinsel and paper decorations such as I had never seen, toys galore, crying dolls and dishes–anything to gladden a small child's heart. He had to leave the parcels in the boathouse until the children were in bed so as not to rouse their curiosity. I had more fun watching Wentie open the parcel and listening to him giggle when a doll cried "Mam-m-ma", than I had watching the girls open their own gifts.

Wentie felt we were doomed for a severe winter. He made a rough sled in the form of a stone boat. He fastened four pieces of logs, two feet long, on it. Each time it snowed he hauled the rig down the path and back again. He had a good road and a scenic view through the woods to the boathouse. An old fisherman came by and said, "by damn, that's the finest bit of shovellin' I ever did see. How did you do it without shovel marks?

Several of Wentie's brothers and friends came to see us during the holiday season and took back word that Croucher's Island was the most Christmassy place they had ever seen.

On February 11, 1923, more than fifty people walked to the island; twenty-five of whom visited the lighthouse. Among that group was a Mrs. Oliver Dauphinee, now deceased. In Mr. Croucher's forty years on the island, he said that he had never been able to walk ashore.

Someone asked Wentie how he liked the island. He said the island was fine, but the weather was horrible. "It's my first winter. I guess it will also be my last one here".

That year there was a potato famine. Everyone grieved about the poor crop. Wentie dug ours, and we had enough to last 'til March first.

Wentie seemed to know how to do everything. The children and I looked up to him. We were very happy in our island home. However, after so many people walked to the island in February, I wanted to go see my mother. She lived five miles distant, and I had often skated much farther. In 1917 I had dislocated my left ankle and had not worn skates again. I was undaunted over a mere five-mile trek.

On Monday I did all my housework and fixed a lined box on the sled for the children so they wouldn't get cold. I wanted to get away early Tuesday morning.

As the old folk said, "Man plans but god displans"! So it was on February 13, 1923. The morning broke dull, and I had my misgivings. Wentie came in and said, "I wish you'd give up the idea of going to your mother's today". Even as we talked the day seemed to darken. Soon after a little snowflake passed the window, quickly followed by another. By noon there were rifts in the ice; the wind howled, the open water was black, building a frilly little white cap on it between the rifts of ice. By 5:00 p.m. all the ice in St. Margaret's Bay was chewed to a mush up to Clam island, which is two miles further inland than our home.

That night I was quite content to sit in the safety and comfort of our fireside with my children and a husband who had the wisdom to know it was dangerous for us to leave home that morning.

Winter passed on peacefully. Wentie could get to the mainland once, sometimes twice a week or perhaps each ten days; much depending on the weather for we only had a very leaky rowboat.

The first boat we had was an old thing that was there when we arrived. It was so rotten that you could almost step through it. With his experience as a sailor, the one thing Wentie would not put up with was a boat that he considered unsafe. Wentie knew what he wanted–a boat with a sloping bow that would be easy to pull up on the slipway.

We applied for a new boat. There was a local boat builder who understood what Wentie wanted and agreed to build it for the princely fee of fifty dollars. The government, however, would have none of this and arranged to have it built in Shelburne for forty dollars. While we waited, we borrowed a boat from a local fisherman. By the time the boat was finished the ice in the Bay was too heavy for the supply vessel to get to the island until the next spring. All that waiting for a savings of ten dollars. When it finally arrived, It was a heavy, hard to handle thing that Wentie never liked. Fortunately it wasn't built any better than it handled and didn't last very long.

The kitchen floor in the lighthouse was worn out and hard to clean. I sewed jute bags together, glued and tacked these to the floor and put on several coats of paint. We were comfortable and cleaning was easier to do.

The Master of Ceremonies of one of our local radio stations produced a five-minute series at 11:55 a.m. called Life. Oh yes, we had a radio. It took an 'A' battery (equivalent in size to a car battery), two 'B' batteries (about half the size of the 'A'), and a 'C' battery (about the size of four 'C' flashlight batteries) to operate it.

I had written to the Master of Ceremonies and was told that he used my letter for one of his subjects. I did not hear it, but I was told it met favourably with the public.

Later, the editor of the *Daily Mail and Star* wanted me to go meet the announcer, but the contact was never made.

Wentie built a hand sleigh and used it to bring non-perishable supplies and mail at ebb tides. It was too treacherous getting on and off the ice at high tides. Each trip was a new revelation for us waiting at home. Even a five-cent box of raisins as a treat for the children meant happiness. It really meant Daddy was thinking of us at all times.

Then there were days of reading and trying out new recipes, for we subscribed to many magazines. Every Sunday Wentie cooked up a pot of molasses candy. He made it so perfectly and often that we even had a hefty, useless pair of scissors reserved for no other purpose than cutting candy.

The boathouse was built on the eastern side of the island. It was the only good place to launch a boat. The fishermen also used our launchway.

In the autumn of 1923, Wentie cut logs and poles. I do not know how he ever dragged such huge things to the shore. With them he built a very large launchway, which included six planks that he had bought to lay from the water's edge to the boathouse. It was easier to unload our boat from this vantage point.

A lovely black pup had been given to us, which we named Gip. On one fine day in March, Wentie was clearing a patch of land on which to build a small pigsty. Ethel, almost three years old, played nearby. I wanted to go out too, so I dressed Geraldine, who scampered any and everywhere before she was a year old. She was now nineteen months old. I told her to play near the door, while I washed the dishes. I looked out later—no Dean to be seen. I called to Wentie and asked, "Did you see Dean'? He answered, "No, but you go to the shore on the other path'. He "skee-daddled" one path, as I ran the other one. Wentie got there first. He found the dog near the water, which was rolling up in a white foam. Dean was on the plank kicking the dog, saying, "Dit, Gip, Dit"! Gip was our protector and friend for a number of years, until she went feeble and blind.

Finally, March first came and we had no potatoes! Unbelievable! How would we survive? We still had plenty of flour and yeast, so I could bake big loaves of fluffy white bread. So, for a whole month, I'd fry steak one day and boil sauerkraut in the lard the next day. Everyone was well. We were young and happy, with the hope that the next day would be different. If it wasn't, there was still another day coming. Nothing to fret about.

The ice was so thick, the sea would crack it and the wind would force it inland by day. Then it would be calm at night and drift back to open sea. The creaking and groaning at night was so severe a body could hardly sleep.

Wentie made little hand sleighs for the children. As they grew older, he made larger sleighs for them. He also made a handbarrow, which we used together when it got too slushy for the sled. Often I couldn't come when he needed me, so he made a wheelbarrow.

And so we spent the winter on Croucher's Island.

Chapter four

When spring came we cut rockweed and carried it up for a garden. Wentie found that to be a slow effort, so he built a rack on the wheelbarrow. One could scarcely see his head above the load of rockweed. I still wonder how he did so much.

The garden we made at the door consisted of small vegetables. Potatoes, turnips and mangels he planted on his brother's place on the mainland. There Cliff loaned him his horse and machinery to cultivate his garden.

When digging on the island, Wentie found something that always had him wondering. It was made of iron, hand constructed. Although he showed it to many people, none could suggest a use for it.

It had a six-inch central ring with, at one time, eight spokes welded to it at even intervals. The spokes were about five-eighths inch diameter, seven inches long and sharpened to a razor-blade keenness. One spoke was broken off, or missing, when he found it. Wentie had built boxes, benches, chairs, bureaus, tables, cupboards, boats, dinghy and paddles, a barn, pig pens, chicken houses, fences, and broke and sank rocks, but he never found a use for this gadget, nor could he name it.

Just about any and everything grew on the island. Each spring the children were each allowed to select a package of seeds to plant and tend for their own pleasure. We had such wonderful honeysuckle, spirea, climbing rose and wygelia. We had a vast variety of bulbs and other flowers too numerous to list. There are three, however, that I would like to give special mention. The ivory – colored evening sweet pea grew such as I have never seen before, or since. They were so pale and perfect they looked like wax. The Japanese forget-me-not, the most perfect little beauty that ever grew, but when it went to seed it became the peskiest thing that ever grew. There was a seed for each petal, about fifty flowers on each stem. The seeds were raspy and stuck to one's clothes. We tossed them out like weeds, but still they grew. The portulaca, a ground-covering plant, which, I think, is sometimes called the Christmas Rose. When well fertilized it's greatest height is eight inches, but it's multi-colored blooms were beautiful. I've spent many dollars on portulaca seeds since leaving the island, but never raised one plant. Wild portulaca or Creeping Charlie takes over gardens on the mainland and is a rarely used food plant.

We were all very fond of apples. Wentie sent for apple and pear trees. These included three Wagner, three MacIntosh, two Gravenstein, and one Sweet Bough apple trees and two Clapps Favorite pear trees. The trees grew well on the island but, strangely enough, were not very productive. The pear trees grew most rapidly, had excessive blooms, but no sign of fruit.

Wentie wrote to the Experimental Farm in Kentville, Nova Scotia. They sent us scions of the Bartlett pear tree, explaining that two trees of the same name would not pollinate each other. After Wentie grafted the trees, there were delicious but scant productions of pears. He bought one dozen gooseberry bushes and grafted some wild apple trees with very good results.

The children were taught to know and eat the raw vegetables from the garden, such as radishes, peas, beans and rhubarb. Around 1935 we even had a successful crop of peanuts. Unfortunately, we roasted them too much so they were not good to eat.

I read an article in a magazine that told how you could get two crops per season from one garden plot. Wentie was often skeptical about my experiments, but chuckled his way along with me.

Somewhere along the line Wentie found time to order boards, one inch by four inches, and posts to build a wonderful fence around the flower garden. Many people said it was larger than their vegetable gardens and others compared it to the Public Gardens in Halifax, except that the spacing between rows was on a much more limited basis. Wentie also made a rose trellis and an archway for the honeysuckle to climb. He liked all flowers, but his pride and joy was a velvety white rose, Sir Thomas Lipton by name.

There were no hardwood trees on the island. In later years the children planted both dogwood and maple, and both flourished. The variety of flowers was too numerous to mention. There were only two snakes on the island and one of these was killed by Mr. Croucher. Wentie got the other, "a whopper", in the same place many years later. No toads. We tried to raise some but they did not survive. No mayflowers either. Quite a few moles, one rat, lizards galore and also red ants.

Cows. Well, cows have shapes, sizes, colors and personalities; just like people, and people have their own opinions about cows. In July, 1923, Wentie's brother, Cliff, had a cow for sale. Who would be the most likely person to buy it? Wentie, of course! His poor little children had no milk. That meant build a barn!

The fishermen weren't very happy with the prospects of a cow on the island. Domestic animals love to roam on the shore and can destroy nets left to dry. Wentie bought fence posts on the mainland, cut poles on the island, and built a fence over half of the island to keep our cow out of the fishermen's gear as they cleaned and repaired it on the shore.

Wentie never swam a cow to, or from, the island. He always rigged two boats together, which made a steadier transport. He was always kindness itself and I never heard him raise his voice in anger.

Mr. Croucher knew how necessary the remainder of the island would be to a lightkeeper, and he refused many would-be purchasers in favor of Wentie.

As previously stated, Wentie looked to economy. Even so we kept a plain but wholesome table—one in which cows and hens played a large part. I could soon slap a meal on the table for one or a dozen people.

On the island we had fun planning where to dig up a new spot for gardening or which area to sow down for hay. The children and I did most of our gardening on the Government side, while Wentie, the children and I worked his part of the island, including the pasture. He always saved the refuse from the lobster pots and wheeled it to my garden.

Just as we kept a wholesome table for ourselves, so did Wentie feed the animals. We couldn't raise enough hay on the island. We preferred buying loose hay to baled hay as we found the latter to be of poor quality. Sometimes we had two cows or a cow and a young animal. It was another of Wentie's virtues that he required two of everything to prevent loneliness in the barn.

Usually we were able to obtain hay from neighbors on the mainland. Once the hay was on the island, it still had to be carried up to the barn. This was done with hay ropes. Wentie bought a coil of small rope, cut it into desirable pieces and seized both ends. These ropes we referred to as hay ropes. Woebetide the offender who used those ropes for any other purpose. He laid the ropes in a certain way, loaded on the hay, pulled the rope up around the hay, tied the hay in securely and off we headed up to the barn. We usually put about thirty-three pounds to each rope, which, though not heavy to carry, made a cumbersome bulk on one's back. None of us complained, because it was like playing a game. Each was proud of being able to show how much he, or she, could do.

The children each had their own ropes, which held a lesser amount. As Wentie used to say, "a pound is a pound, and it all helps".

I never went in the boats for hay, but always helped unload and carry it to the barn. After the island hay was made and new grass had a chance to grow, Wentie would put a fence around my garden, and we would let the cattle in on the Government side as the pasture was getting low in feed.

One year I had an abundance of Westerfield and Yellow

Denver onions, which I carefully tended for drying on a large wooden flake near the doorstep. Would you believe it? That one old cow sneaked up and ate a quarter of my prize onions. No way could we keep her from them1 there was just no stopping old Poppy, one of the nicest cows that we ever owned.

Franklyn, Wentie's brother, had a cow, perfect in performance, with only one bad fault. His real reason for selling her was that he had to change his place of residence. Where he was moving, cows were banned. Franklyn truthfully told us Pansy would not give her milk down without a little lick of shorts (cow treat). A quarter of a cup would do the trick.

The rule in our barn was that no animal got store-bought feed in June or July. During the remainder of the year they were treated to everything, which could include mangels or green oats in season. Wentie was going to teach Pansy who was boss, and "Pansy", like the unpredictable female, met his challenge.

One bright Sunday morning Wentie sallied forth to milk Pansy, who apparently in the right mood, gave seven quarts of milk. I don't know if it was that they were both in the same mood or what the reason, but as time progressed Wentie found himself fighting a losing battle. One day he came to the house mad as a hatter with one pint of milk in the bucket. Old Pansy stood in the barn softly moo-ing "Told you so"!

'Twas a beautiful morning, and the poor old cow really wanted out, so I said, "let me try her". Wentie said, "go ahead, but no shorts! Without them you can save yourself the trouble". He sulkily sat down to breakfast, while I took the milk pail and went to the barn. I talked to Pansy and petted her a bit, then sat down, stuck my head in her flank and began to milk. She gave me her milk freely. I soon returned with a foaming full pail. She would not give milk to Wentie again without food. He was sure that I gave her a treat to get her in the "giving" mood.

Some years later Wentie went to Hammonds Plains to buy a cow. I don't know any name to call that critter. She was ugly, ill shaped and starved. Her milk was bitter, with almost no cream. I churned for three days and never got a slick of butter. I don't remember what Wentie did with her, but I think he put her out to pasture and then likely sold her to a butcher, the only thing that he could do.

Some years later, he bought two sick, starved animals. It was a bad year for farmers. They couldn't feed their cattle well. Those cows would eat rockweed from the shore as they ate hay. After their desire for rockweed lessened, they put on fat, but their performance as dairy cows was nil. One made a few pounds of butter; the other made non-beatable-quality butter, but not enough to cover her keep.

Wentie went to western Nova Scotia to visit a farm in Lunenburg County. There he bought a small cow. How I did like that old red Rose. She was not a heavy producer, but the quality was super. And so goes the story of some of our cows. You can really make pets of them.

In later years, when Wentie got assistants, I did not do so much work outside. Their coming made more work in the house for me. It meant more cooking, washing and mending. We were very crowded in our old, leaky lighthouse. Even though they tried hard to make repairs, one south window persisted to leak, and this soaked our beds in heavy storms.

The only machinery that we had on the island were the motor boats, which seemed easily acquired on demand. Of course, I had my sewing machine, which I had bought while Wentie was overseas and brought to the island with me. After fifteen years we did get a hand-operated washing machine, but there were no tractors or machines of that sort.

Each year we broke a patch more of ground. We hoped to raise enough hay on the island to feed our cow. It was hard work boating hay to the island from the mainland. When clearing the land, we rolled the rocks away. For any rock too large for us to roll, we'd dig a big hole beside it and push it in. This we called "sinking rocks".

Chapter five

During the early 1920's Miss Agnes McPhail became the first female elected to the Legislative Assembly in Ottawa. It was about this time that the miners in Cape Breton went on strike. Newspapers were full of pathetic stories of the hardships that they suffered. The Honorable Miss McPhail was chosen to go to Cape Breton to assess the destitution suffered by those miners and their families. Honorable McPhail surely was a good journalist as well as a compassionate investigator. One could use a crying towel, while reading her reports.

One of her statements, which angered me, was "The dear little children wore dresses made of flour bags". My children were also dressed in clothes made of flour bags. I was proud of it and never felt demeaned using this type of cotton. When those bags were bleached, dyed in the color of your choice, embroidered and trimmed with a touch of homemade lace, the children were well and comfortably dressed.

One set of dresses, in particular, was dyed burnt orange with little black bunnies embroidered on them, and these were much admired by visitors. Thus we utilized the humble flour bag. People spoke openly, conversed freely, saying things that may not occur to them in ordinary places. Some remarked about the beauty of those dresses saying that they didn't see anything like them in stores or catalogues. Even yet I'm not sure if they were jeering at, or complimenting me.

I made nightdresses, pyjamas, slips, aprons, blouses, pillowcases, sheets and tea towels. Bags cut in strips, dyed, joined with alternate white strips and quilted in a fancy pattern made an attractive quilt.

The bags were sewn with one fine thread and one coarse thread. When ravelling or opening these, we wound the thread each to its own size on separate balls. I'd sew the required number of bags in the form of a sheet. Wentie would mark an 'X' at desired intervals, then pick up the 'X', wrap ten times around it, in the tie-and-dye method. The children called this style the doughnut quilt. The quilting pattern really showed those quilts off. From the fine string with which the bags were sewn I crocheted a child's sweater. Waste not, want not.

One summer Lever Bros. supplied me with Rinso, Lifebuoy and other soaps for testing their product. When folks saw how pure white my bleached bags were and asked what kind of soap I used, I'd reply "Rinso". They'd say, "O C'mon", and laugh until I showed the package. I usually made most of my laundry soap. Fish oil made wonderful soap, but it gave a horrible odor.

Wentie knew that I was very much interested in any kind of needlework. He often saw little gadgets (needles, pins, and threads), which he knew I'd use; so he would bring some home for me. One thing that he never dared to buy was a crochet hook. Those were too testy. Sizes varied. Even I had to make several swatches to get the right tension. With his understanding and my willingness to learn, we mastered the art of tatting (a form of lace making). In our first years on the island he would cut quilt blocks and rug rags for me in exchange for my helping him with the outside work.

When I needed knitting needles to make fine lace, Wentie made them from the spokes of a bicycle wheel. When I needed larger needles, he made those from heavier wire found inside roofing paper rolls.

We bought binoculars. The first binoculars were bought from T. Eaton Co. for fifteen dollars. One day in April, 1924, at daybreak Wentie saw something huge, indistinct, south-southwest of the island. He continued watching it and spotted two men rowing a large boat piled high with something. Those men were having a hard pull and were glad to get beyond Indian Point into French Village, where the sea was slightly sheltered by Macdonald's Point. Next morning Wentie went to work in the boathouse. He found a strange boat in the launchway and two chilled men sitting in the sand trying to get warm. He asked them to the house. I offered them breakfast, which they refused. They were taking blocks to be sawn into shingles by a man who had a mill at Frost Fish Cove, Glen Haven. The wind blew too hard for them to return home. They had to spend the night with the mill owner's family. Next morning they hoped to get ahead of the wind, but could only get to Croucher's Island. We gave them dinner and supper and offered them a night's lodging, but they felt the wind was abating. They set out for home.

Wentie loved to read, knit nets and make small boats and oars. He also made a canvas hammock which, for years, hung in the area on the southern end of the island that we called the Park. It was an area where we cleaned up big trees by removing lower limbs and then cleared out the underbrush. We were protected from the wind and yet the sun could beam in to its heart's content. When the canvas hammock wore out, Wentie knitted a hammock and put it up near the front door for our two smaller children and our grandchildren to play on.

Wentie also played the violin in the evenings. I loved to sing, the children humming along with me, as I knitted and listened to "show me Mother, show me". I made their clothes, quilts, and rugs. I also crocheted. There was always some activity, such as carrying wood and water or washing on the old scrub board. One day I was hanging out clothes. Wentie came in and found Ethel, two-and-a-half years old, laying the table; while Geraldine, eighteen months old, was standing on a chair by the stove testing the potatoes for doneness. Another day I returned to the house to find the wash tub laying on its side on the kitchen floor. The rugs were floating around. Oh, how they helped!

When the children were small, Wentie would take them on his arm to a tree where the mother bird would be setting on her nest. He talked quietly to the bird and the children. When mowing, if he'd see a bird fly, he'd look carefully and find the nest in the ground and leave hay to protect it. The children would get another nature lesson.

He knew all the birds, even on wing–their habits and where they built their nests. He had a better education than I, but not the ability to teach.

For the present, lighthouse keeping on Croucher's Island was a learning experience, but darned hard work. I do not recall anything unusual happening for the remainder of 1924, except that I got pregnant! Our little one was due January 23, 1925. New Year's Day Wentie said, "You better get ready to go ashore". I replied, "No hurry"! He said, "You don't know what the weather will be like. I don't want you here without help."

I had previously made arrangements with my sister, Grace (Mrs. Hiram Smith), Tantallon, to take the girls and me; while her son, Vincent, thirteen years old, would bring his books to stay with Wentie on the island.

Her older son, Lester, often spoke of how much firewood he had to cut that winter. I just bet that he wished Aunt Maggie had had her babies in the summertime. However, Lester was still able to take time out to smoke a sheet of glass black to look at the sun in eclipse.

Our first son arrived on Saturday night, January 31, 1925. Everyone was happy for us.

OUR FIRST SON

Three times I'd entered the Valley
Of the Shadow, so they say;
God had given us two little girls
Blithe, bonny and gay.

The third time I entered the Valley
To us, a son was given
Pink, dimpled and smiling
Truly a gift from Heaven.

Life on Croucher's Island

'Twas a cold, cold night in winter
The wind blew down nor'west
But my heart was warm with loving
As I fondled our son to my breast.

We christened him Bertram Graham
T'was a good name for our son
It was the name of his Dad's buddy
When they fought in World War One.

We watched our darling baby grow
As he played with his sisters sweet
For he was only ten months old,
When we heard his pattering feet.

He'd crawl on chairs, and climb the stairs
He'd even scale the wall
He'd tumble down, but try again
Undaunted by his fall.

We bought him toys, which we thought best
But he'd say AGAIN and AGAIN,
Don't you know, what a boy wants most
Is a GREAT BIG AEROPLANE!

We lived in an island Lighthouse
The children could not go to school.
But at the kitchen table
They learned the Golden Rule.

Now Bertrum loved to study,
At reading he did best,
Nature, history and arithmetic
He ranked high, in any test.

Maggie B. Boutilier

He'd roam the shore and field alike,
He learned much in those hours.
And fill his pockets with stones and bugs
But bring me pretty flowers.

Time sped by as if on wings
Now, Bert was a stalwart lad
With a Mother's pride, I adored this child
'Cause he was a pal for Dad.

But not for long, did he tarry home
For the din of World War Two,
Echoed a challenge to our boys
And Bert donned the Air Force Blue.

With hidden tears, beneath our smiles,
We bade our son good-bye
For he must go so far away
To train, and learn to fly.

He studied well with the other lads
Navigation was his aim
And when the war was over
He came flying home again.

He loved to serve his country,
And joined the R.C.M.P.
Now he's on the West Coast
Rescuing ships at Sea.

This is the story of our First Son
Whom I call "li'l feller"
He has three sisters who bring us joy
And a slim, blue-eyed brother.

Grace had a Dr. Miles' calendar hanging in her kitchen. Naturally each page contained many advertisements, a cure-all for all ailments. When she turned the page to February, in big letters at the bottom of the page it read, "DO YOU FEEL TIRED AND PALE?" Grace said, "I'll really be glad to see February go. I'm so tired of seeing that face me, I'm beginning to feel that way."

When Bertram Graham was three weeks old, Grace and I took him to St. Margaret's Church and had him baptized. Reverend I. E. Fraser was Parish priest at that time. On February 23 the three wee ones and I returned home to the island.

While we were absent Wentie had his first attack of appendicitis. He also developed a mild case of Psoriasis on his right leg, which had been wounded during World War One. In spite of this, Wentie had been busy cutting firewood and splitting it up in the woods to be carried and wheeled home next summer. There wasn't much snow in the winter of 1924-25. What snow there was didn't pack solid.

On April 10 I dressed the girls and told them to go where they heard their father cutting. I busied myself with household chores. All too soon I heard a small child pounding on the door. I answered. There stood Dean crying, "Effel is 'tuck in a 'no bank"!

I quickly ran down the path. There was Ethel in the bank, one leg only, up to her hip. I took her under the arms and pulled, but I couldn't budge her. I soothed her with kind words and rushed to the boathouse, quickly returning with a hoe. I had to dig carefully so as not to injure her. You'd never believe how fast she was held there.

After examining her for injury, and finding none, I sent the girls on their way. I returned to the house where three-month-old Bert was sleeping soundly. I felt so refreshed from the crisp air, I attacked the delayed housework with new vigor, but it was past noon ere I got my clothes on the line to dry.

In the spring of 1925 Wentie got the use of a motorboat from a fisherman, whose father kept the Post Office and a general merchandise store at French Village. He was not interested in either of these. He loved fishing and made it his life's work.

Wentie was not a consistent fisherman—only if the moon, tide and bait indicated a good run of fish. One night I said to him, "I'd like to go to Grace's tomorrow". He replied, "I'm going fishing in the morning". "That is fine, but you leave the lighthouse boat (a large rowboat) for us."

The morning was beautiful. Wentie went fishing. After the morning chores were done, I put the three children in the boat and started to row. I was really scared, but I had to show my mettle. A great need may arise sometime. I wanted to be sure that I could have confidence in myself. It was only about three miles to row.

I was scared of one shoal and a certain rock on it. We went inside the rock with the motor boat at high tide, but outside at low tide. I wasn't sure just where it was. I saw that ominous thing to the right of me, lightly covered with water and was as frightened as if it were alive and would attack us, so I pulled hard and fast on the oars.

Ethel said, "Mother, why are you rowing so fast"? I said, "I may go into the rowing race at the Labor Day Picnic. I'm just practicing". I didn't want to scare the girls. Bertram was too young to understand.

Grace's husband, Hiram Smith, was a much sought-after sawyer and worked anywhere from Nova Scotia to Quebec. His coming and going depended on the quantity of logs to be sawed for his term of service. He just happened to be home the day of my adventure.

How happy I was to be met by him. He asked for Wentie and I told him that Wentie was fishing, but that he would come for us. Hiram just couldn't believe I'd come such a distance with our little ones. It is always sloppy in St. Margaret's Bay in the ever-prevailing southwest wind.

When Wentie returned home, he dressed the fish, ate his dinner and came for us. He was as surprised to see Hiram as

LIGHTHOUSE

I'd like to be a lighthouse
All scrubbed and painted white,
I'd like to be a lighthouse
And stay awake all night.
To keep my eye on everything
That sails my patch of sea;
I'd like to be a lighthouse
With the ships all watching me.

Hiram had been to see the children and me. Wentie always caught fish for our own use and had some to share with our relatives.

The old timers usually planned their work, such as fishing and planting, by the moon and tide. One day I heard an old fisherman say, "You can count on a run of mackerel every eight days". I asked, "Why eight days"? He replied, "Because of the moon". Personally, I really think there is a lot of wisdom in it, because I have since seen things affected by moon phases.

It was early in August, 1925, when fishermen from Boutilier's Point and Indian Point set their seine one beautiful Saturday morning. That night a real storm blew up, dragging anchors and graplings, snapping the moorings and bunching the nets so badly that the men could not set either the spiller or the sweep.

The men knew there was trouble even before they left their homes to come to the island. They felt that if the wind would abate and the whole crew was there, they might be able to reset the gear enough to keep the fish quiet until the next morning. They seldom took out fish on Sunday.

Time was fleeting, nearing suppertime. They dreaded the long row home and back. I said, "Give me some fish and I'll rustle up a snack for you". I got the fish and hurried to the house. Seeing Wentie's drawknife on the hook, I grabbed it to make a quick fire. As I shaved kindling with the stick against my knee, I thought that I must be careful and not cut my knee as my brother, Lawson, had done. Zip! The deed was done and the blood flew.

I wrapped a towel around the injury and proceeded to boil potatoes and fry fish. There were plenty of sweets in the pantry for dessert. The men were amazed when the children called them for supper. The girls were four and five years old, while Bertram was only seven months old, so the men knew that they hadn't helped me with the meal.

After supper Wentie fed the pig and hens, then milked the cow before going to the shore. As I cleaned up the supper dishes

I realized that I was losing too much blood. I sent the girls to the shore to tell their Dad. One old fisherman said, "My God, she's cut an artery. Wentie, come with me to get iodine"! They went to the mainland. Wentie had asked another man to put up the light. I didn't know that he had made this arrangement, so I went upstairs and had the lamp ready to go up the last flight when the man came. He shivered so badly when he saw the blood; I almost refused to allow him to take the lamp up.

He was a long-time friend of our family who loved our children and brought each of the girls a small basket with a doll in it, a blond for Ethel and a brunette for Dean. He never enjoyed good health from birth to the very end. He had over sixty operations, losing his right arm somewhere along the way. He did beautiful needlework of various types during the last twenty years of his life; yes, with only one arm!

When Wentie returned, Iodine was poured into the cut on my knee to help stop the bleeding and prevent infection. My leg healed over quickly, but festered inside, breaking out in two places below the scar. Perhaps the bone was shaved for I removed two splinter-like pieces from the openings. The children said, "Mother is always smiling, even to her knee". It was rough going for a few weeks.

In 1926, Wentie's sister-in-law, Mary, spent a few weeks with us. She was pregnant, and she and I were working on her first layette. Ethel and Dean, six and five years old, invited her to go with them to see an ant's nest. They wended their way down into the pasture, kicked over a rotted stump, picked up a few lizards and played with them.

Poor, dear Mary came home hysterical, laughing and crying about those crazy kids, that didn't know the danger they were in. The children couldn't understand her concern, as lizard playing was a daily event for them.

Chapter six

Our first chickens were purchased in 1922. There were usually about three hundred kept during the summer. These were sold in the fall to people on the mainland, which reduced the winter flock to one hundred and twenty-five or less. In those days if one wanted chicken for dinner, one took the axe and went out to the back yard to catch a chicken. Most people bought enough chickens to last them over the winter, so there was a ready market for our birds in the fall.

As I experimented with different kinds of seeds, Wentie experimented with different breeds of chickens. We had Barred Rock, Wyandottes, Australorps, Rhode Island Reds, Buff Arpington and Brahmas with feathers on their legs. We also had the Light Sussex, which were the nicest of all, although the Light Sussex – Rhode Island Red cross was a close second. The strangest were the black Australorps. These were huge, jet black, noiseless fowls. When we entered the pen these birds did not rush to meet us looking for food like the other fowl, they just stood silently and waited. When Wentie took them to be sold, the storekeeper's son asked him where he got the turkeys. We only tried these birds for one year. They were hard to dress for the pot and too big and silent for our taste.

Wentie's brother, Cliff, and his wife, Laura, had a mixed farm in Glen Haven. Their prime interest was dairy, selling some fresh milk to the summer people and shipping cream to Bridgewater. Their poultry business also began to improve, until they were handling chickens by the thousands. Business was flourishing and Wentie was in an ideal spot to supplement his salary, so he built another hen house.

One morning he arose early, took two rowboats behind the motorboat and went ashore to get lumber. He was detained longer than he intended. The wind came in from the southwest and his trip home was rougher than expected. He anchored the motorboat south of the launchway and unloaded the first boat. "Now", he said, "you must come out and bring in the other load of lumber". "Yikes!" I thought. He, with all the confidence of an old salt, rowed the boat out and made it fast to the motorboat. He saw me safely seated in the second boat of lumber, headed for the launchway with orders to watch the sea; if the surf was rough, troll the boat out until the sea made its third run, then it would lull.

When I looked down that shoreline and saw a mountainous white wall of water coming, I threw all caution to the wind and thought, pull–pull as hard as you can! The first lop raised the rear of the boat and lumber high, the second drove me crosswise against the shore, and the third put me high enough on the skids that I was able to pull in the oars and grab the painter to make the boat fast. Meanwhile, Wentie was standing in the motorboat, chewing tobacco, waving his arms and yelling, while three frightened little tykes stood in the launchway crying, "Mother's going to drown". I guess at no time was I in any danger; it was just that I was panicky and disobeyed the laws of nature.

Wentie took the motorboat to the club, made it fast and came in with the other boat—making a perfect landing. As we worked unloading my precious load of lumber and securing our boats, Wentie continued to explain to me the virtues of right and wrong. I said, "Okay, let's do it all over again now that I know how"! He replied, "Hump! A Man is only wasting his time trying to tell you anything". At this point he, the children, and I picked up a load and headed up the hill, where Wentie was soon busily engaged with his carpenter tools.

Some years later, when I was returning to the island from a frequent hospital trip, Wentie tried to land the motorboat in the launchway so that I would not have to transfer from one boat to another at the club. The wind was strong from the north. Only a few boat lengths from the launchway the motor clunked out. Bert was waiting for us and had the presence of mind to run down the shore. The boat was still carrying her speed from the motor, but the wind carried us speedily along. Wentie acted quickly. Coiling a rope, he let it fly at Bert, who missed; so Wentie coiled again and sent it flying in Bert's direction. At risk to himself, Bert plunged into the surf and caught us, thus saving us a long, cold night at sea, for that is where a north wind would have taken us.

Late in 1927, we had an old red rooster. One day he attacked Bert. Ethel and Dean came to his rescue. Old Red held us all at bay from time to time to Wentie's amusement. The children and I were talking about it at the table. Wentie said, "He knows better than to tackle me. Once would be it'!

Shortly after Wentie was going through the yard with a small roll of roofing paper in one hand and a box of tools in the other and, BANG, he got it in the legs. He turned to meet Mr. Red, challenging ego for ego. Wentie spanked him with the roll of paper, until the old bird gave up the chase. Wentie declared that he won't do that again! Ha, ha–says who? Mr. Red looked for a fight until the axe took his head off.

Like any good farmer, Wentie was always looking for strange, or new, blood in the flock; so he sent to Ontario for setting eggs. Each egg was stamped with a symbol. The eggs were okay, but the brood hens were very unpredictable; however, with tender care, we fared quite well with the fluffy, plump chickens.

We kept a handsome Plymouth Rock rooster for our mixed breed of hens, apart from the pullets. I never did discover if Mr. Plymouth did not like his residence, feeding, watering, or his wives, as he was also ill natured. In fact, he was as cranky as he was handsome.

One day he flew into the old dog, Gip. She ran him around the lighthouse so often that all he could say was "Cook, cook,

cook" as he feebly ran. Even that didn't hold him for long. One night I went to gather eggs. WHAM—I got it in the back! I turned and kicked the beast. I drove him under the nests. He shook his head and gnashed his beak, only to charge again. This time I aimed him for the door leading into the hen yard, where he sauntered to a big rock crowing his head off as if jeering at me. I don't think we even made a soup stock of him, but I really can't remember his fate.

As the children grew, they were all taught to help, inside and out. The poultry business kept all of us busy. It meant moving tons of feed up the hill. Wentie felt one hundred pounds was too heavy, so he made several trips to land a bag. The hard work seemed to make Bert grow all the quicker, so by the age of fourteen he was as tall and strong as some men. At that age he could, and did, carry one-hundred-pound bags of feed on his shoulders from the shore to the feed shed, which lay between the barn and the pig sty.

We did not keep so many hens and chickens in the winter, but still our hens laid more eggs than we could use. One day Wentie started out with eleven dozen to trade for small staples at Burchell's store in French Village. Due to the treacherous condition of getting on and off the ice, he had three dozen saleable eggs on arrival. Some of our friends had an abundance of eggnogs, omelettes and scrambled eggs for a few days.

Chapter seven

In 1926 the little girls only had me to romp with, in a scatter-brain fashion. Dad played quietly, but I was too reckless at times. When Bert was a year old, the girls teased me to go coasting with them. Where to find time—but I must. I got an old fashioned pot of beans ready, dressed the children, put Bert in the wash boiler and fastened it on my sleigh. I tied Ethel's sleigh to mine and Dean's sleigh to Ethel's (toboggan style) and hopped on behind Bert. All I needed was a whip to crack and we were away. We didn't get far, when I heard a yell. A glance over my shoulder showed Dean, spread eagle. We then thumped over a hump or drop of land, where we lost Ethel. Bert and I continued on at a furious pace with the snow so glib that I couldn't stop. We landed in a bunch of bushes and rocks. I was momentarily scared. When we scrambled back to the girls, I was happy to hear them say, "That is enough of that'!!

Anyway, it was an outing and very refreshing. We returned to the house to hear something sizzling on the stove. I picked up the bean crock to push it to the back of the stove. I stood there with the top of that precious pot in my hand, beans flowing over the stove and floor. Glory be!

In my haste to please the children, I must have forgotten to heat the pot thoroughly before putting it on the stove. The bottom was sliced off as cleanly as if it had been done with a glasscutter.

We had our good times on the island. True, I would get tired of the constant care of the children. On Sundays, when

Wentie was home, I'd take a book and sneak away for a quiet hour under a tree. My solitude was all too abruptly ended when I'd see a faithful old dog and three tiny tots standing before me. The children would say "Go find Mother, Gip", and she would lead the way. I then graduated to the hayloft for relaxation. It too was eventually found. Oh well!

I always made birthday cakes. Wentie's favourite cake was gingerbread, but for his birthday he got the same plain white cake as the rest of us. What made his day, June 19, so special was that the children and I would scrounge the island for a dish of wild strawberries just for him—his favourite berry. He even preferred it over the tame strawberries. No one, no, not one person could find these berries as Wentie himself could. He found them where others could not see them or thought they'd been picked.

As the boys grew older, their preference was for chocolate cake with white icing topped by one-half of a walnut per serving. When each child reached the age of ten years, they made their own birthday cake. One day one of them made a chocolate cake. He forgot to include the flour. Land sakes! Talk about good fudge!

On special days the good dishes were taken from the top shelf to give a party air to the day. If eats were a little slack for supper, a pan of hot biscuits, fresh apple sauce and a daub of cream served in the dishes from the top shelf satisfied the pangs of hunger and took the drabness from the meal.

Our children didn't have much opportunity to attend the usual children's parties ashore. One day in particular, a Sunday School or Church picnic was in progress. Wentie was busy with the fishermen. There was hay to bring in and a storm was brewing. I said, "Never mind children, we'll have our own picnic"!

We hurried and scurried. We got the hay in and I polished the stove and scrubbed the floor (it's surprising what an added comfort a mere dusting and a bit of scrubbing gives to an old wooden floor) and made a cake, which I baked in a nine-inch by twelve-inch pan. Then I made a pot of butterscotch candy, put a thin layer of icing on the cake, allowed the children to make balls of candy, stuck a tooth pick in each ball and put the other end of the pick in the cake. I then announced "We have a LOLLY-POP cake. Wonder what kind they have at the picnic?"

By this time it was raining quite hard and it was cold. There was a knock on the door. Seven young boys and girls stood there chilled to the bone. As they draped their clothes over chairs to dry and propped their feet as close to the stove as each could get, I served warm drinks; the children passed the cookies and "the cake".

I said "There now, children, you did have a picnic after all". The guests chorused "a picnic! I wouldn't have missed this for any picnic I ever saw"! I don't remember who the children were.

At Halloween the children helped me make cookies in the shape of cats, brooms and pumpkins. We used currants for eyes and shredded coconut for facial features.

One nice day I was upstairs house cleaning. I could hear the children slipping in and out of the house. What could be sweeter; they, enjoying the outdoors and, me, knowing where they were. I'd call downstairs–"What are you doing?" "Playing house Mother."

When I came down to get supper, I was minus about three dozen molasses doughnuts and a jar of cookies. I said, "What in the world did you do with all that food"?

"Mother, when you have company you always serve a lunch". Gip and Dinah, the cat, were their guests so they fed them until they could eat no more. The doughnuts had been sliced like little round cookies. By the way, the children didn't want any supper–I wonder why?

A favourite snack of my childhood was sour cream and molasses, or sugar, to dunk our bread in. Of course, it became a rare treat at the lighthouse too. One day I put the two girls in their cribs and went out for strawberries. When I returned I was met in the doorway by Wentie saying, "You didn't save much by going out". I can see that awful mess even yet of sugar in the cream bowl, over the floor and cream in the sugar bowl. What could I say! Such a mess to clean.

This one still has me puzzled. Bert was so fat that he rarely hurt himself. He walked when he was ten months old and climbed everywhere. Wentie made a gate to keep Bert from climbing the stairs. The latter was equal to a leaning ladder. The gate was up a step and was hinged flat on the steps. I think Bert was about fifteen months old. I put him to bed and went to the garden.

I can only guess that Bert got out of his crib, climbed those stairs and fell down. The only bruise we could find on him was a crescent shape on his forehead, distinctly the shape of a picket on the gate. He just had to tumble far, and hard, to receive that imprint.

Bert always sang before breakfast, all day and through his life. He is almost fifty-eight years old at the time of this writing, and he always enters his door singing or whistling.

When I asked Wentie if we could get a gramophone in the lighthouse, he said "We don't need one; you sing all the time anyway". We eventually got the gramophone. All our children sing though none are trained singers. Half way between the barn and the northern end of the island there was an extremely steep bank with a deep depression (a basin-type of thing), then another slope to the shore on the western side of the island. One did not dare to use a sleigh there. Heavy rains filled the basin. The children would watch and pray for the water to freeze, but it would only make a shell ice on top, which tinkled like music played on bottles when broken. The water leaked out somehow.

Alas, alack, how the seats went out of those children's play clothes on that bank when they got big enough to travel by themselves. With or without sleighs, they would slide.

Chapter eight

Wentie subscribed to two daily papers: the *Evening Mail* and *Daily Echo*. When the children began to read and write, they enjoyed the "Children's Corner". "Farmer Smith", editor of the *Evening Mail* (a post that I believe she held for forty years) was responsible for the building of a home to enable under-privileged children to enjoy two weeks of vacation. It was built at Cow Bay, in later years referred to as Silver Sands.

It seems to me that the *Daily Echo* also had a different name. However, it too had a children's feature, which was under the supervision of "Cousin Peggy". This feature was called the "Sunshine Club". Our children gained many pen pals by writing to other children, some of whom are life-long friends.

Contests were run in the paper, which also included recipes, drawing and story telling. I do not remember each of the prizes our children won, but Bert did win a camera and a dog. With the camera he crept up on birds to get s picture. He also loved snowfall and sugar-snow scenes. One sunny day he took a picture of a fire out of control in Black Point, a distance of more than a mile.

The dog, an English Bull Terrier donated by a kennel club in Bedford, Bert called Flip. I often felt like flipping her when I had to mend five pairs of Bert's pants and seven of his shirts in a five-month period.

One day he was demonstrating the dog's intelligence for his uncle. The hatchway from the kitchen to the cellar was open. Bert was backing up and–WHAM–down the hatchway and into the cellar he went. He came up with nothing hurt but his pride, no bones or skin broken anywhere. The kennel owner eventually bought the dog back, not because we didn't want him anymore, but because he was needed for breeding stock.

The Sunshine Club purchased a property on Mason's Point on the shores of Schooner Cove as a recreational home for its underprivileged children. When the paper discontinued printing, the place was bought by the Anglican church for a youth camp. When it was still under the supervision of the Sunshine Club, Wentie, the children and I would visit and bring some things from our island garden. It was a nice place to give a large squash.

We never really had much time to play. Usually our leisure was spent in learning to do needlework and perfecting the stitches we knew. My mother had given Bert a piece of flannelette for Christmas. I made him a shirt. WHAM–first time on, a rip by the dog! I said, "Young man, if its fun to tear 'em up, find out how much fun it is to mend 'em". I pinned a patch in place and seven-year-old Bert tried the fine art of stitchery. With tongue in cheek and pulling the thread out of the needle, he struggled on. After an hour, he said, "Here it is Mother, but I don't think it is very good". Not bad for a start, but not good enough. "No son, I don't like it much either. Let's do it over again." Next try better, but still not good. He said, "Know what? If the girls can sew a quilt, I think that I can too."

The girls had previously taken first prize on a quilt at a Halifax Exhibition. Their quilt was nursery characters on white blocks embroidered in red, put together with turkey-red in a windowpane style.

The girls were now working on a similar quilt in blue and white. Bert got his quilt block. Three strands of floss was rather much for a little boy to handle. By the time his third block was finished, it was very good. So, again, the children took first prize. The organizers suggested they try an entry of a different type of work another year.

The first quilt I made on the island from patchwork was called the "Maltese Cross". It should have been very pretty, but, as a matter of fact, it was very ugly. When working with a variety of colours in making a patchwork quilt, one should make the block pattern by using as few colours as possible. I did not know that, so I mixed the colours. Old Timers called it "hit and miss". Believe me, I missed one hundred per cent on that venture.

Another quilt was pink water lilies and green pads appliqued on blue sateen. A young lady voiced her objection to the green with blue. I suggested that she study the flowers in the garden and she would find that most blue flowers had green foliage. None were undesirable or lacked in beauty.

The most interesting quilt I ever worked on was called the Snowflake Quilt. I only ever saw one other beside my own. That was at a county fair. Although the quilt was a finished product, the pattern was incomplete. I once read that no two snowflakes are identical. That was certainly the case in this quilt pattern.

We subscribed to a magazine, *The Family Herald and Weekly Star*, which had a section for every need. In 1932 a snowflake pattern was printed in the needlework section. For fifteen consecutive weeks one quarter of a snowflake was printed. The quilt maker would turn that quarter over on paper, creating a complete snowflake by tracing a quarter at a time. Then the pattern was transferred to blue broadcloth and embroidered with white floss. I never saw so many different stitches in my life. You were supposed to do a block a week. After five blocks my work was placed in a box for two years due to pregnancy.

When Wayne reached the toddling stage, he was forever into my snowflake quilt box! At long last I got the twelve blocks embroidered and then made the fifteen-inch band of white, which was to represent the heavy snowfall. That was as far as the quilt on display at the exhibition went, but we couldn't let ours look lie that–too unfinished! However, without Wentie's help, it would have been left that way.

A road must go on the snowbank showing horses' tracks and another shade of blue casting shadows where evergreen trees blocked the sunshine. I was not keen enough on figures to weave the road or cast the shadows, but clever Wentie fathomed it to perfection and cut a pattern.

Oft times I'd serve a meal and sneak away to pin a foot or so of road in place. Not for many moments could I escape our little Wayne. One day he hopped down from the table, rushed in and buried his little face in the quilt, leaving a stain that I could never remove. I carried them both beneath my heart at the same time. They seemed to belong together, and they are—the cherished quilt is now in Wayne's home in Ottawa, where many people admire it.

I made so very many nursery quilts. Not tiny baby quilts, but in various sizes better defined as children's quilts. One that stands out in my mind was a white background with a child, appliqued in blue, picking flowers near a pond. Her name and that of her home were embroidered on the quilt. Years later I was a guest in a young lady's home. Her father was showing home movies. I was familiar with some of the scenes, but when that quilt flashed up, I gasped. I never realized it was so beautiful. To see my handiwork in pictures thrilled me.

Another quilt of interest was the nursery rhyme "Little Boy Blue". Each letter was large and embroidered in blue cross-stitch on a yellow background. Each line was illustrated with a suitable drawing; such as a boy in blue with a horn, or a sheep in the meadow. This quilt is also in Ottawa.

Another unusual quilt was "Little Bo-Peep". Again a white background was chosen. I did not know there were more than five lines to the rhyme, but found about twenty lines.

Again the pattern was designed on paper, and again it was Wentie to the rescue. He helped me plan the size of letters; the distance apart; and the placing of verses, which were illustrated by the use of hand drawings. The letters were a full inch deep, embroidered in chain stitch in shades of pink. A lady remarked that she never knew two people who could work so much alike. It made the work look as though it had all been done by one person. Wentie printed the first four lines and I completed the printing.

We decided that this quilt should be for our first grand-daughter, where the quilt can be seen today. This quilt was sent to the Atlantic Winter Fair, but was not exhibited. Because of its unusual design it apparently was felt that nothing could compete with it. Each of the quilts described were sashed all around with appropriately coloured material to give a framed picture effect.

Meanwhile, Bert learned to do very lovely embroidery. One day I admired a pair of pillow cases in a mail order catalogue. Bert asked me for two flour bags, which I bleached in quantities. Of course, I thought his request unusual and queried why two bags? He pretended it was nothing important, but he took the girls into his confidence. Christmas morning a very pretty pair of pillowcases were under the tree for Mother from son Bert, worked in my favourite colour of pink. He hid his work well for I hadn't the faintest idea of what was in the making. I adored my gift for none knew better than I the hours of labour of love that went into that fine stitchery. He never lost his desire nor ability to do needlework, just broadened his knowledge.

Chapter nine

Ice cream—we all love it, but I almost learned to hate it. Early in our life Wentie bought a three-quart ice-cream freezer. In late October, we could find enough thin ice to freeze ice cream. The high bank, densely wooded with spruce trees, protected the ice on the western side of the island until late May; therefore, for a full six months, each Saturday, I had to make ice cream. No matter how many cookies, pies, cakes or other concoctions I experimented with, "Huh! No ice cream!!"

I tried every recipe that I saw and often failed, but we did not know that the amount of salt used in the freezing was an important factor. The favourite recipe was caramel, which requires you to melt one-half of the sugar. It had a flavour all its own. Then, of course, there was the argument about who cleaned the dasher last week and whose turn it was to have it this week. When the family moved ashore where they could buy ice cream, I refused to make it at all.

Wentie was always buying new tinsel and tree decorations. One year, he bought two beautiful tinsel ducks, but he also bought little Bert a gun about a foot long with a string attached to a little cork. When the trigger was pressed, POP went the cork. Harmless, but kids will be kids.

One night I went to tend the light, while Wentie went to do the stable work. Ethel told Bert to shoot a duck like Daddy does. He was too little, so they dragged a chair up to the tree. POP! Off comes the duck's head with the remainder hanging prettily on the tree.

I said, "Your son likes shooting ducks, and he is a good marksman too". Dad said, "HMMPH"! It's still debatable who was most to blame in the shooting incident, Ethel or Bert. A few nights later, Wentie started out at dusk to hunt ducks. He thought there was more noise than he usually made. He looked behind him and there was Bert with his gun on his shoulder, planning to join the hunt.

The first few summers Wentie wouldn't allow me to help him carry the drums of oil to the oil house. In 1926 he asked me to help him. We put down a track of lumber, two-by-fours, for smooth rolling. While he and I held the drums against the slope of the hill, Ethel and Dean carried the two-by-fours ahead to form the track for us. It was hard work for each of us, but we would work together as though playing a game, trying to see who could do the most. The girls were six and five years old at this time. Chubby Bert was nineteen months, holding my skirt. Before Wentie allowed the children and I to help him roll the oil barrels up from the landing to the oil house; the oil was carried up five gallons at a time.

Although Wentie would not get treatment for himself, he was so compassionate when others suffered that his anxiety rendered him helpless in time of stress. He always complained about poor health, but would never see a doctor. Often, when he went on business, usually to make a purchase, the lady of the house would treat him to a tasty glass of wine. He would ask how the wine was made and was then given the recipe. I made each and found them very tasty: Apple Wine from a lady in Boutilier's Point; Rhubarb Wine from another in Harrietsfield; Dandelion Wine from my sister, Grace. I believe each of these to be a wholesome, non-intoxicating drink if taken as a treat. Wentie never used hard liquor anyway.

Some of his friends suggested he use Stout as a tonic. Nothing helped him for long. When despondent, his greatest uplift was a visit with his mother and brother, Cliff. Deep within me, I often felt sorry for him. He had a dual personality, some days the wonderful loving man I had married and suddenly, a complete stranger. All too late, I fully realized he was suffering from War nerves.

Through the summer of 1926 Wentie seemed more weary

than usual. On January 2, 1927, he said, "Can you help me put the boat in the water? I will slowly paddle my way to Indian Point. Maybe someone will take me to the Village. I must see a doctor". The doctor sent him to hospital for x-rays.

Wentie's father, Albert (age 74 years) was chosen to stay with the children and me on the island. Gran'dad was a gravedigger and prided himself on the quality of his work. Hilbert Grono, 27, died December 30, 1926, and was buried in St. Paul's Cemetery at French Village on January 2, 1927. Gran'dad wouldn't allow anyone to finish his work, saying "They'll be alright on the island for one night, and I'll go back out tomorrow".

Next morning, January 3, the fish buyer came by to purchase lobsters that Wentie held in the fish crate. He was a good, honest man. His boat was too big to come ashore and he didn't want me to go to the crate, so he lifted the fish, put the money in a mitten, and threw it ashore to me. He needed a rock to give it weight. It fell short of its target, but I easily recovered it, giving us all a hearty laugh.

Gran'dad arrived mid-morning. After that I had no more outside chores to do, not even carry a bucket of water. You see, the island was not equipped with today's modern conveniences. Our water was hand carried from the well; lights were kerosene lamps; our phone was yelling at the top of one's voice on a calm day to fishermen, who relayed messages.

Gran'dad cut firewood. The dear old soul would come home with a large stick on his shoulder and his axe in his hand. He loved apples for a nightly snack.

Gran'dad asked me where I got my spare bed. I told him it was a spool bed Wentie's brother gave to him. He said, "I knew it. It was the bed Mother an' me bought in 1875". Later, Wentie cut it down for a single bed. We still have the bed in storage.

Wentie came home, still uncomfortable. In a few days word came; hurry back to hospital–an operation was imminent. He was taken to hospital and operated on the next day. Gran'dad returned to the island to stay with the children and me. He kept cutting firewood.

The days proceeded as usual except that we had bought two cords of hardwood and, while Gran'dad continued cutting softwood, I wheeled several loads up the hill each day to get a supply in the woodshed before Wentie came home. That type of work would be a definite no-no after an operation. When Gran'dad left I had all the work to do, inside and out, as well as tend the light. Wentie was forbidden to climb the stairs or lift the hatches for three months.

People with small acreages usually began getting rockweed in March to replenish the quality of their soil for gardening. One morning Wentie saw two Kennedy brothers, each in his own rowboat, coming from the Ingram River area. They passed by the island to cut rockweed on the shore of Indian Point. The wind blew northwest gales all day, which was dead ahead against them. It was too rough even for our motorboat.

Wentie, with his marine experience, watched anxiously all day knowing that those men could not get home without assistance. He felt they had spent the entire day without food or water. At nine o'clock that night, in a big broad moon, he said to me, "I think the wind has gone down a little. Do you think you could help me get the boat out and meet me when I come home?" Mission completed. Those men were very happy to be helped. It put new life into Wentie too. He became more lively and ventured forth as normal for the first time since his operation.

One day during the summer, some visitors arrived at our launchway in a neat little motorboat. The boat was for sale. Wentie said it was too small, but later took it on loan for winter use and eventually bought it. It was much easier to haul in the boathouse out of storms. Hauling was done manually, with the assistance of a winch. I usually operated the winch.

The winch in the boathouse that we used to haul the boats up the slipway was a four-to-one reduction. This meant that for every four turns on the handle, the winch drum turned only once. How many, many times I turned that handle during our years on the island.

Later on, Wentie wanted a larger boat for summer use. We

bought a beautiful boat, twenty-four feet long with a six-foot beam. It really cut capers in a summer breeze. We could not haul it in or out. We had to lay it at anchor and use a tender between island and anchorage. We always had a group of friends help us to get the *Mermaid* on land in the fall. Usually, a group of young lads from Tantallon helped put it in the water in May. Finally, Wentie's mother's teacup reading came true.

Wentie was always messing around with his boats, trying out something to make them either more beautiful or useful. One Saturday something was bugging him, a leaking stuffing box, I think, or perhaps a change of engine bed. He said, "Do you think you and the children could help me land the boat"? I said, "That's a big order. The children are so small, but we'll try".

Wentie always seemed to have each move planned well in advance. Away we went to the shore and, "By Jingo, we made it!" "Don't go away for I'll need you to pass things to me".

We stopped for a lunch. The children and I did a few noon chores, then went to the shore to help Dad again. It was very late afternoon when we slid the old *Mermaid* back in the water. Wentie went to the village for a trial run, while the children and I went to a dreary, unclean house.

As I kindled a fire, I said, "Oh, if I had some apples, I'd make a pie for supper". Bert said, "I get you some apples, Mudda!" He grabbed up his little basket and left.

The girls were doing little chores. I said, "Oh dear Lord, where is the baby? Run quick and see if you can find him!" They came running back to me saying, "He is over the hill crying, but we can't find him!" With my heart in my mouth, I sped on flying feet. That child was tip-top in the highest wild apple tree on the island, holding on to his little basket of apples. I said, "Dear, you must throw your apples down", as I kicked off my shoes to climb the tree. He wouldn't throw the apples, but I had to, as I wrapped a strong arm around my little son and edged my way down that big tree, even though I was afraid of slipping.

By the time we got back to the house, it was time to put

We set out for the island in Wentie's pride and joy, the "Mermaid".

the light up. And so had gone another day, in what some folk thought to be the uneventful life of a lightkeeper's wife. The outdoor chores were still to be done. Bert never ate a cooked apple and did not care for pears in any form; however, he loved radish.

We had used the radish from near the oil house, and I had transplanted cabbage there. One special cabbage was doing extremely well. I watched it daily with pride. One day Bert came up the hill, utterly disgusted. He held up my prize cabbage and exclaimed, "Look Mudda, they ain't one d**n bite on it"!

Although Wentie enjoyed privacy, he could only endure solitude for short periods of time. When I saw him stuff his left hand in his trouser pocket and pace the floor, I could expect to hear, "I'd like to go ashore. If I can't make it, I can always come back"! I saw that happen to him just once.

The requirements for the upkeep of the boats seemed endless. Wentie's knowledge, gained as a sailor, was a boon to him in lighthouse keeping. Each spring the club pole and attachments had to be scraped and painted. Then, they had to be attached to the club rock and the whole lot set out where it belonged. In the fall the whole process had to be repeated in reverse. The boat was kept in the water from mid-May to late

October.

The club's most important feature was its anchor or "club rock". Not all rocks are suitable. The rock must weigh several hundred pounds, be flat on one side and rise thicker to a bowl shape on the opposite side. A hole is drilled in the center of the rock and an eyebolt inserted. On one end of the bolt is a small eye, which just fits through the drill hole. A cotter pin is then inserted to keep the bolt in the stone. The hollow in the stone allows it to sit on the ocean floor without the cotter pin touching. This not only allows the stone to sit flat, but ensures that the cotter pin will not be damaged by the weight of the stone or by the seabed should it drag. At the other end of the bolt is a large eye with a swivel and heavy chain attached. The chain length varies according to the depth of the tide. Fastened to the chain is a long wooden pole or "club" about eight inches in diameter, which floats above the surface. A hole is drilled about six inches from the top of this pole and a crosspiece is inserted. It is to this crosspiece that the boat is tied. The great advantage of the club pole is that it floats vertically in the water with the tie-point at a convenient height. Thus, one does not need to lean over the side of the boat with a boathook, fishing for a mooring line. It is especially convenient at night or on a rough and windy day.

Wentie would say "Get the children ready, we are going to haul the club rock in today". I would reply, "Do they have to come? They are so small", or "It is so cold". He would reply, "They can each pull a pound"!

Away we'd go with ropes, block and tackle at a certain tide. It seemed that our lives were ruled by tides, sun and moon. I do not recall each and every move, but Wentie knew just when each move required the least effort. The children and I asked no questions, we just tried to understand, and do what we were told. Sometimes it was good enough, other times not quite right.

Wentie had two club rocks during our twenty-two years of service. One time we did not pull it high enough on the land. During the winter it froze in the ice. On one very high tide, the ice was carried away and our rock went with it. When a group of men worked together, they sometimes made weights from cement, especially in later years. The real old-timers made killocks that took three men to lift, half killing all of them.

As I think of things now, I marvel at how much work Wentie did and yet he'd be gone away so much. On one very beautiful day, he was gone. I never missed him, except while watching for him to come home so that I could be ready to help haul up the boat. The children and I were always happy to meet him. It seemed like a break in daily routine.

On this particular day, I had washed clothes and then used the rinse water to clean floors from lantern down to wood-shed, including the doorstep. My little tykes came in and, in a frightened tone, said "Mother, there are four black men in the yard"!

I went out and spoke to them. I found four white men, so greasy that they were pitiful, but also pleasant and well mannered. They were out of the engine room of the last ship to ever take freight from Miller Bros. Sawmill in Ingramport.

The ship's name was *S.S. Hilfern* of Scotland. The men were the oilers from the engine room. The ship was leaving next day and they were testing the lifeboats for leakage. They did not want to go upstairs to see the light, because they knew they'd leave marks, but I insisted they have the grand tour and avail themselves of the same hospitality we'd always shown to others. They were most congenial, interested in every frivolous item. They even preferred the hit-and-miss rag rug to the scenery mat made of wool. Meanwhile, Wentie came home. He took them through the gardens, his workshop, and other areas of interest.

The Chief Engineer was from Ireland. He told one of the younger lads to eat a piece of sourdock to quench his thirst when walking. The young chap was a Portuguese, who rubbed his tummy and edged away, saying, "No, no"! If the others were foreigners, they did not say. They were very young and shy. The older gentleman told Wentie, "We'll be going out tomorrow at 2:00 p.m. Come to the western side of the island

and wave us goodbye.

Again the day was bright. All five of us went down to the bank. When that handsome ship passed, we got three loud blasts of the horn. Wentie's ego went up in leaps and bounds. He said, "That's a salute–a very high honour. Those men must surely have taken back a good report about us, for only the Captain could order that recognition"! We were overjoyed. I gladly washed the footprints made by those men and have many happy memories of that day.

It would be impossible to record all the enjoyable instances spent with visitors, but some will appear for time to time.

One day in 1928 I took the three older children fishing for perch near the shore. I still didn't know two cents' worth about a boat but was always willing to call a bluff, and finally did learn a little about them. The wind blew southwest quite lightly, but in that great expanse of water, even a light breeze seemed rough. I was really too afraid to go far from shore, and then didn't know how much rope to play out to give the graplin enough to lay flat on the bottom. We began to fish anyway. As we fished, I watched our boat drift up toward the reef off Woody island. We weren't catching any fish, but I was too scared to pull up anchor for fear the wind would carry us faster than I could row. I surely was stupid. We finally got home alright. Wentie knew we were in no danger. It turned out that he was keeping an eye on us all the while.

Another warm evening, we again went fishing. It was oil calm, the water was ebon black, the sky was also very dark. We anchored south of the fishermen's seine. We caught a few perch and flatfish, which one old fisherman called "sand dabs". Dean hooked a wriggling fish that played the line this-a-way and that-a-way. She hung on; we didn't have a gaff, but finally landed a basket skate. We all yelled and screeched so much that our old dog, Gip, came barking madly. She jumped in the water and swam to the boat. We helped to pull her in. Dad came, fearful and breathless, grateful that it was only a fish that caused the hullabaloo. The fish was a hideous looking thing. We talked of it often.

On August 18, 1928, the children and I again went fishing. Wentie came rushing to the shore, calling us in. He said, "Miller's Mill is on fire. (This is commonly known as the Ingramport fire.) Let's go up". We went up and laid some distance offshore. It was a dreadful sight to behold–a financial loss to the owners and the community as a whole. Many men depended on employment with Miller Bros. for the support of their families. Older men, as far away as French Village, would get excited about loading deals, when the ships were in. When Wentie's father was almost seventy years old, in 1919, he would walk about one-and-one-half miles around Frost Fish Cove, out onto Indian Point, catch a boat with other men and row two miles more to work loading boats for ten hours. Returning at night, he hoped that one of his sons would meet him at Indian Point, so that he should not have that tiresome walk back home.

One night nobody was available to take the rowboat out. Wentie's mother asked her daughter-in-law, Sadie, and me to go for Mr. Boutilier. All either Sadie or I know about a boat was that to make it go ahead–you pulled on an oar; it was really laughable. As the old folks said, one of us stroked today, and the other stroked tomorrow. We arrived a met a very happy, old Dad, who said that he would row home. I don't think he could have stood our shenanigans.

Another fire will always remain strongly imprinted in my memory. It occurred on October 9, 1944, when lightening struck a house in Glen Haven. The damage was rather extensive. The same storm set his brother's barn on fire. It was a complete loss. The same bolt may have been responsible for both fires as the two brothers lived next door to each other.

Chapter ten

In the autumn of 1928 Wentie seemed to weaken. The cold caused him such suffering and uncontrolled shivering, the pallor of his face was pathetic to behold. After a few weeks the problem would settle down, all would be normal again.

Between Christmas and New Years he contracted the 'flu. January 2, 1929, I made a fire on the northern end of the island. No-one saw it.

The children took sick next. Bert begged me to hold him, but the chores were piling up before me, so I refused his request. Soon, I noticed him doing strange things. I said, "Wentie, quick get a bucket of water in the wash boiler. Heat it to body heat and put in some mustard"! Bertram was going into convulsions. I don't know if that was the cure, but I dipped and dried him, put him in bed with warm bricks and a cold cloth on his head. He was better in a few hours.

January 3, some of Wentie's brothers came, guessing something was wrong, because Wentie hadn't been ashore. That night I took sick. Next day Wentie flew a flag from sunrise to sunset. Not a soul saw that flag.

January 5, Wentie got ashore and phoned for my sister, Grace. She came to Seabright by bus and from there someone brought her to the island. She stayed until January 8. Wentie took her to Boutilier's Point, where they flagged the train to bring her to French Village Station in Tantallon. As Wentie's dad said, winter wasn't long after that.

The remainder of the winter passed uneventfully, except that I was worried about the children's studies. True, I had taught them to read and write, but I had memories of things in school that I was unable to teach them.

Wentie's brother, Willis, has had my undying gratitude throughout his lifetime, and I'm still grateful. It was he who guided me to the Nova Scotia Technical College (NSTC), which, at that time, was responsible for correspondence courses. It was a wonderful find for the children and me.

Wentie also knew it was good for the children and was often in the house during lesson periods. The oral work greatly disturbed him. During our play sessions, our noise and laughter unnerved him as much as if we were crying.

We didn't have much furniture, nor was there room in the lighthouse for much. Wentie had made me a very useful sewing cabinet, but drew the line on school desks. He got so interested in fishing and associating with the fishermen that he sometimes overlooked the household needs and my requests.

When Bert was twelve years old, he liked a quiet place for his studies and reading. In those days boxes were made of wood. Biscuits could be bought in twenty-pound boxes. I took two of those boxes, spread apart for knee-hold space, and nailed on a few boards. Alas, the boxes weren't high enough to accept Bert's knees, so I had to cajole Wentie into putting feet on the boxes with two-by-fours. Painted, with a nice piece of table oilcloth on top, they made a comfortable desk to work on.

A similar clothes closet was made for the girls' room from orange crates, with a broom handle to form a hanging rod. This was covered with wallpaper, inside and out, and with chintz drapes, on a stout wire, to cover the front opening. It created a nice place to keep the clothes tidy, including the shoes.

This brings two proverbs to mind: "I'll find a way or make" and "Necessity is the mother of invention". What a humble invention, but it was most necessary in my case.

As necessity is the mother of invention, I took a small table, two wooden boxes (which had contained window glass), stood the narrow side on either end of the table and between them I placed a biscuit box (which just spanned the space to

The men get a lesson on the finer points of splitting wood.

each of the smaller boxes). I nailed the works together, gave all a coat of paint, and we were in business. At least one child had a place to work and a handy spot to keep the books. When Wentie saw that I'd find a way or make it, he made a bureau for each of the bedrooms. We still have those neat bureaus.

One Saturday Wentie asked if we would like to go visit my mother on the following day. Oh my, yes, we would. Sunday was clear and beautiful. Wentie tended the light, then went to the outside chores. I staggered to the bedroom door and asked the children if they could get breakfast for themselves. I was subject to painful headaches, and this one was so severe that I can almost feel it as I write.

The day wore on, with hope against hope that Mother would soon feel like travelling, but when 2:00 p.m. came and I was still in bed in a darkened room, the children knew they wouldn't see Gran'ma that day. Bert took his little basket and a pair of small scissors. He filled the basket with roses–stems about one inch long, threw the scissors on top and said, "Here, Mudda, 'mell dem an' you'll feel betta"! I don't know if that turned the trick or not, but I was able to help serve supper.

Chapter eleven

The chief industries of St. Margaret's Bay were fishing, lumbering and shipbuilding. When the first white settlers came to St. Margaret's Bay in 1752, its waters were very full of various species of fish. Even in Whynacht's Cove, one of the innermost inlets, food fish such as mackerel, herring and gaspereau, eels and salmon were easily caught. Eel pots were fashioned from withrod bushes (referred to as " withs") and set in the salt water; while weirs were set in rivers, where speckled trout were also plentiful.

Meanwhile, it was the fishermen's policy to offer a chance to the lightkeeper to fish with them, if he chose to do so. There was a fair share per man, if fishing was good. One never knew what the fishermen's luck would be. As I recall, over the years, it was always a dream to put more money in the bank than we took out. It's amazing how much hard work, heavy lifting and expense a man puts into fishing, and often doesn't get enough fish for dinner.

Prominent businessmen saw fishing as a good investment. They approached the more diligent men of the area, who built homes and cleared land for their families as their best bet for survival. Such men as these were asked to put up their homes for collateral. When unable to meet the prescribed commitments agreed to, their homes were forfeited. Many a good man lost his home under the terms of agreement.

Wentie's grandfather was one of those unfortunate victims. Any man who had money enough to properly set himself up in the fish-gear business wouldn't need to work. He could live

The fishermen haul a net. During our stay on the island, this was a frustrating and unprofitable occupation. The only "gold in them thar waters" must have been fool's gold.

off the dividends from what he had already earned. It was a case of the rich getting richer and poor getting poorer.

Fishing was still good through the nineteenth century but at the turn of the twentieth century, it began to fail. Rum running began to pick up. Fishing was just a sham for the most successful and daring runners.

The older men were discouraged. After the fall of Wall Street, they grew weary and resigned to the fate of the "Hungry 30's". Most of the individual fishermen gradually sold off their gear, which, in many cases, was as weak and tired as they were.

At the lighthouse we listened to the tales of the old fishermen, of "when thar sure waz gold in them thar waters"!

Wentie liked a challenge and thought that if we kept fishing, we would also find the pot of gold at the rainbow's end. Then, too, there were so many men out of work–maybe he could buy up the old fishing gear. It would make work, and they would be rewarded with a harvest of hope.

Everyone was alert, listening for a bargain for Wentie. Often, when he went ashore he heard of a seine, spiller, sweep,

lead net or such, but, of course, each one needed a little repair.

All this twine needed a seine boat that was very large, a spiller boat and one for the moorings. Then each man, who would fish with us, would have a boat or two; two seines were needed. When one seine got dirty or torn, usually by constant flowing of tide or storm, it must be replaced to catch fish; while seine number one was being cleaned, tanned and re-paired.

Cleaning up required a bark pot and puncheons. In olden days wood was cut and peeled, the bark was steeped in water like strong tea and poured over the nets and ropes to preserve them against the salt water.

One day Wentie came home excited. He said, "Hurry up—get dinner over. We are going to take the children up to see your mother"! (Something must be in the wind.) Coming home he said, "We will stop at Oakland Point. I heard of a bark pot for sale there".

A genial, retired fisherman met us. He spoke well with a good sales pitch, but, for once in Wentie's life, he saw that the object he sought was too heavy for his needs. It was a huge pot requiring about six staunch men to handle it.

Nearby was the largest vat I had ever seen. I feel sure the sunken vat was equal to a hold in a small vessel. Surely several seines, moorings and a tarpaulin could be bathed all at once in this outfit. When Wentie refused to buy the pot, the elderly gentleman looked at the children and me and jokingly said, "Mrs., that would make you a fine pot for soup", to which I retorted "You should know. You had the brood to feed it to"! I knew this was true, because he had seventeen children. We parted cordially.

Next we visited a fish store on Mason's Point, where a seine boat was for sale. The boat was not of standard size, but it was so well painted it literally shone. Once again we faced a fluent salesman, who gave a real sales pitch on the value of a good boat in a fisherman's life. Wentie knew wood. He removed his jackknife from his pocket, put the blade into a plank in the boat, replaced the knife to his pocket, talking about boats in general and casually said he didn't think the boat would qualify to meet our needs. The owner said, "she's a good looking boat, all painted good". Wentie replied, "Yeah, take a woman to a beauty shop and paint her up, she sure is pretty, but it doesn't mean she can work". When we reached home I asked Wentie why he didn't buy the boat. He said the wood in it was so soft it wouldn't last one season.

Finally, we got enough patched-up gear and unemployed men to cast their luck with ours. The seine was set in high hopes of a rich return. Daily, weekly, for months those men diligently tended those nets in disappointment, catching so few fish it didn't pay them to peddle the small number from door to door.

Nearing late autumn, the men grew listless and didn't show up for days at a time, but Wentie doggedly kept up the watch alone.

One morning, he came in and asked me if I could help him at the shore. (Poor soul, his body was growing weaker at this time too.) I went down to the shore with him. In his boat lay the only swordfish I have ever seen. I'll never understand how he got it in the boat unscathed alone, but I soon learned how to handle it from thereon, until it was taken away from the island.

The fish was a perfect specimen and dressed out to one hundred and forty-nine pounds. We put a tarpaulin shade over it, while Wentie constructed a shipping case, in which he packed it. I helped him get it into the motor boat. He took it to Ingramport Station and sent it off to Boston on the train.

Wentie was ecstatic over the size and perfection of that sword. He exhibited it with pride to all comers, refusing to part with it to anybody, always hoping to put a handle on it. His dreams never materialized.

In 1938 my sister, Ellen, and her husband, James C. Vert, who were ranching in Alberta, came to visit relatives and friends in Nova Scotia. They stayed several days with us on the island. Jim, having been born in New York State, wandered to the Canadian West in early boyhood. He was accustomed only to the far-reaching prairies and was astounded by the miracles of the sea.

We had a hard job convincing him that he was holding and admiring a portion of a fish. He tried to buy it. Wentie couldn't bear his pleading any longer and gave Jim the sword with one stipulation. When he no longer wanted it, it should go to our youngest son, Wayne, who now lives in Ottawa. As near as I know, Wayne still has the sword at the time of writing. Wayne is a collector of relics.

The fishing adventure proved to be a very expensive one. Wentie never gave up hope, until his failing health forced him into selling what he could and giving away the remainder of the fishing gear.

A fisherman's life is rugged and time-consuming. It must be constant, including Sunday. The wet twine is very heavy. The oil skins, later replaced by heavy rubber suits, may keep the ocean water out, but wearing them heats the body, so some prefer being wet by the water rather than by sweat. The hours are from before sunrise to after sunset. Then, if your body strength holds up, you sit in the kitchen (usually the whole family joins in this work), knitting sheets of twine to replace damage done by an occasional large fish, which usually makes several large holes before it escapes.

As told by the friendly fishermen, in olden times people watched each other's house lights. Due to thriftiness, kerosene was as carefully watched as we use electricity today. If a light burned in a different room of a neighbor's house for long (many evenings), some good friend was sure to notice. After supper was cleared away, the kitchen lights were put out and the family gathered in the living room to play games, knit, have a sing song, then evening prayers and early to bed.

At Boutilier's Point, a small cove separates two small points of land. Boutilier families lived on each point. One was an old man whose children had grown up and left for adventure elsewhere. He was mending a net. Nightly he sat with a lamp in the window, while his wife sat in the living room with her knitting. Two people, two lights—unthinkable!

The younger Mr. Boutilier was worried. After a few days, he went over to discover the trouble. The poor old man was mending a net and had forgotten how to pick up the back meshes. He continued cutting out good twine. Though he was disgusted with himself, he was most grateful to his friendly neighbor.

Years ago tuna were not considered an edible fish. They were called horse mackerel and albacore, a dread to fishermen, destructive to gear, big and strong. On rare occasions, the foot rope of the seine could be lifted; the fish would see an opening and swim away. More often the fish panicked, causing costly damage to the gear. Those fish, weighing not less than fifty pounds each (called jumpers) and up to nine hundred pounds and over, had to be taken from the gear. They were often towed ashore and hauled far back on to a tilled field by a team of oxen or horses. The fish were then buried for compost.

When we took up lightkeeping on the island, the tuna were a much sought-after fish, both by the fishermen and sportsmen. Only the largest fish dealer had gear strong enough to take them out of the seine. One day the children and I were watching some tuna being taken. One big fellow, approximately eight hundred pounds, jumped into the boat. The men were so shocked that the poor fish regained his decorum and jumped right out again. Unfortunately, he leaped from the wrong side of the boat and was caught anyway. The opposite side of the boat would have meant his freedom. That incident was a standing joke among the fishermen for many a day.

A Mr. Boutilier on Indian Point had a motorboat. A long-time friend and helper travelled with him. It was not unusual for friends to accompany them, so one foggy night three came to the island. One decided to stay the night with us, the other two started out in a pea-soup fog.

Wentie and our guest listened and said, "The boys are lost". Many people realized the boys were astray.

So many Boutiliers had nicknames and some resented them. Boutilier's Point is on the north shore of the Bay and has a Post Office, which remains to this day, while Davey's Point (still Boutilier) is in Seabright. At least two miles separate the two points. When the two men would shut off their motor to listen and heard men in Seabright call Boutilier's Point, they'd start their motor and head out to sea.

Wentie said, "My God, they'll never find their way. Let's go after them in the rowboat. Two motors may collide in this fog. Maggie, you blow the old conch three times every five minutes".

Wentie was an expert seaman. They took a lantern and a flashlight to read the compass. When they were abreast of Seabright, they caught the men's attention by calling to them. They told them not to start the motor again, but to keep calling. Wentie found two weary, nervous men and guided them to safety. One man said his inner senses told him that he was going the wrong way. Think of the worried wives at home. Though fishermen's hours are irregular, they seldom stay out until near midnight is stormy weather unless there is a disaster.

The island had five fishing berths but only two of these were fished, both on the eastern side. One was near the anchorage; the second, the most used, lay a bit south of the launchway. The third was at the southeast bend of the island. It was too rough on gear.

A prosperous, well-organized fishing firm sent out an agent to interview our fishermen as to why this particular berth was not fished. The local men told him gear could not withstand the sea. The agent chuckled and said, " You show me the marks for the berth, and I'll show you how to fish it"! Agreed.

Several days later big motorboats piled high with fishing equipment hove into sight. The seines were set and the agent rubbed his hands with satisfaction. Two days later the gear was taken up at a loss of several thousand dollars. No way could anything withstand the continuous surge of water at that place.

The other two berths were on the western side, and only one was fished. Fishing gear is marked so that when they put it in the water they know how much to put out before changing its course. They also position the boats by markings on the land, such as a church spire over a private home or a tree over the corner of somebody's fish shed. I was a long time wondering what this talk had to do with the catching of fish. How could it be necessary?

The above-mentioned berth had a coral reef on its most southern end, which destroyed the nets very quickly. The men with rowboats didn't show much interest in this berth. Perhaps the Ingram River, north of it, caused more turbulence. After a few years, some fishing companies with heavier boats and gear became interested in fishing there. Tuna travelled the western side of the island more than the eastern side.

One night there was a heavy run of mackerel. Prices were low. Harnish's were going to tow the whole seine up beyond the island into quieter water, to hold them until prices got better. Just an experiment.

On Friday at three-thirty in the morning Wentie came in and asked, "Have you anything to eat"? "Only bread. Why, do you want something to eat?" "No, eleven of us do"! He turned and went back to the boats.

I jumped out of bed, gave Bert a bottle of milk, made a fire and paced the floor saying, "What will I do"? I had dressed chickens in addition to my other chores on Thursday, and I was tired. However, I quickly stirred up a gingerbread, a pan of biscuits and a batch of drop doughnuts–cooking each in the order in which they were mixed. I buttered bread, made tea (putting milk in some and leaving others black), put sugar and spoons in the basket with the food and was just stepping into a pair of boots at four twenty-seven to take the food to the shore, when Wentie and four other men walked in, hungrier than ever–and cold! September's frost can be bone chilling. They stayed to get warm and eat, while Wentie took the food to the rest at the shore.

When the men tried to move the seine the fish chafed each other so badly they were a total loss. I don't know if it was the huddling of the fish or the noise of the motors that panicked them.

A few weeks later a similar occurrence took place, but this time with codfish. The men came without dividers in the boats. The seas were too rough as the fish would all slither to one side and capsize the boats. Once again, I didn't have much food on hand. One chap said, "Don't worry, Mrs. Boutilier, if you haven't got it, you can damn soon get it. You proved that to us".

For a few years Wentie would ask a bachelor or a strong teenage lad to lobster fish with him for approximately three weeks in December. They'd fish in the morning and cut fire-wood in the afternoons. In the spring, March to May, they fished approximately a month. The catch didn't warrant putting the pots out any longer. During the spring session, in the afternoon, they would prepare soil to plant a garden.

Wentie made lobster pots during the winter. I may say here that there must be a proper way to construct, and a certain kind of wood from which to build, a good-fishing lobster pot. He could catch lobsters in the pots he built, but he heard of twenty pots for sale, reasonably priced. He bought them, but never caught one lobster in two seasons' fishing. Those pots were brought ashore and were left rotting on the island.

By this time, fishing was petering out. Different individuals put in irregular settings, but it didn't really pay to use the gear.

One dreary day, there was a horrible noise on the Bay. It sounded like a heavy waterfall. We saw a few tuna jumping in the air. I had made doughnuts and started the children out with a snack for the fishermen, as was my custom when the men were on the shore. The children only went a short distance when they returned. The noise was so terrible that they thought the fish would come after them. The men said that the fish were thrashers, some of them thirty feet long. There weren't any fish in the Bay for the remainder of that summer.

Only once did I help pick up the seine for loading into the boat. There had been a severe thunderstorm in the autumn. A Seabright fisherman had been stunned by lightening and was unable to do his part. I liked what I did and the men were high in their praises. They had worked hard and long that summer, but received nothing in exchange. The end of a golden dream.

Chapter twelve

Wentie's sister, Sadie, and her husband, George Dauphinee, were residents of Lowell, Massachusetts, U.S.A., where he was employed as a mechanic by the railroad. Usually their infrequent holidays in Nova Scotia were made by train. One year they motored home. What could be more thrilling than to treat each member of the family to a day's outing in their car. Cars were still quite rare among the labouring folk in Nova Scotia.

On the mainland, it was easy to say let's go here or there tomorrow, but on the island, arrangements had to be made in advance with Wentie. On October 9 it was go or miss out, as Sadie and George were leaving for home on October 10.

The morning of October 9 was dull and calm. Ordinarily, Wentie would have smelled trouble, but that trip in an automobile, especially with George and Sadie, was a once-in-a-lifetime event. We enjoyed the day in Halifax visiting with relatives and doing a little shopping.

Wind and rain set in as we were coming home. Wentie wanted me to stay on the mainland, but I was insistent about returning to the island with him. We had three little children, with no extra clothes. Why not go home? We only got abreast of Indian Point, when the engine cut out. We had taken in too much water. Wentie took to the oars, otherwise the wind would have beached us at will. He took us to Mrs. Abram Burchell's house. She warmed the children and me, and dried our clothes. Meanwhile, Wentie got one of his brothers and they rowed to the island.

No matter how cold or snowy the winter, there were always chores that had to be done.

About dusk, the wind had gone down and the rain stopped–at the turn of the tide I suppose. Somebody, I can't remember who, took the children and me home. Like the old woman and her pig, we did get home that night after all, but I wasn't very popular for a few days after coming home. Wentie didn't like having his instructions ignored.

November 17 we went to Tantallon, our final run for the season. My niece was visiting her mother (my sister, Maude Manuel). She had three little girls at that time. We brought them home with us. The next morning I awoke with a severe headache. About 4:30 p.m. we had a slight earthquake. Wentie quickly put up the light and ordered everyone to get dressed. I couldn't see the need of us leaving the island. He said that there might be another, and heavier, quake. We should be with other people.

His dear old mother bedded the seven of us down. The next day my niece and her children were taken to her mother's house. Wentie, Bert and I came home to the island. There had been a small tidal wave. Very high tides! Our girls spent a few weeks with their Uncle Cliff, Aunt Laura, and some of their cousins. They came home for Christmas.

Wentie developed such a cough and cold that he was going to give up the island. He drew house plans all winter and estimated costs of building a home and hen houses, enough to give him an income of five hundred dollars a year–he was sure that we could live on that.

We had already deducted several hundred dollars from our salary, which we would forfeit if we quit the island before ten years of service. We talked it over. He seemed less worried, when he saw that I was willing to stay. How little I thought, when boosting his morale in 1928, that I'd be the ultimate cause of our leaving.

Wentie had built a large picnic-type swing, beside the path near the lighthouse. Hundreds of people visited us during the months of July and August. Almost everybody, even the old, felt young when they saw that swing and took a few sways on it.

One day in August, Ethel was pushing some playmates and said she had a sharp pain in her side. It seemed to pass quickly. Nothing was thought of it. 'Mid September the three children suffered a little biliousness. It was just a twenty-four-hour thing for Dean and Bert, but Ethel's lasted several days. Four o'clock on September 18, Wentie said, "Get the children ready. We are taking Ethel to a doctor".

We couldn't leave the island before tending the light, but we hurriedly got breakfast and did the outside chores. The weather was damp, foggy, with a light lop on the water, which the motorboat cut through quite easily. We landed at a wharf near Wentie's parents. Wentie went somewhere to phone for the doctor, who was residing with his family at the Dundella Hotel, where he had an office.

I had accompanied Ethel to her grandparents' home. The doctor advised that we get her to hospital with as few gentle moves as possible. The appendix was in danger of rupturing. Wentie went hastily for George, who, with Sadie, quickly responded. We got Ethel into emergency before 11:00 a.m. The operation was successful.

Wentie's brother, Franklyn, and family came to stay on the island with him, while I was staying with his sister in Halifax. Dean and Bert were staying with my sister, Grace. She, Hiram, and their children, always seemed to be a staunch standby.

My youngest brother came in for me on Saturday evening, as Franklyn's family felt they had had enough of island life. We expected to return to Halifax within the week to pick up Ethel, but the hospital rang up saying that infection had set in and Ethel was asking for her mother. I went for her, once again leaving the children with their Aunt Grace, while her son, Vincent, went to stay with Wentie on the island.

It was 'nip and tuck' with Ethel. The doctors expected to find infection at the time of operating and couldn't understand why it should set in after ten days. I knew an Anglican minister who had lost his only child, a girl of twelve years, in a similar manner a few years previous.

My brother and a young friend came to Halifax in the evening of October 9 to bring us home from the hospital. They had brought Dean, Bert and a cousin in with them for the drive.

Coming home along the Bay Road near Upper Tantallon, the boys saw something huge in the road. My brother, driving, was keeping right. The lad on the passenger's side excitedly said, "Turn left, turn left"! As he spoke, the car came to a grinding halt. We had been attacked by a monstrous Bull Moose. I guess the poor animal was blinded by the lights. It was badly wounded. We reported the accident to the Game Warden, who found the moose the next day. They shot and dressed it, giving the meat to a hospital. It was edible, as hunting season was due to open within a few days. I can't recall how, but we arrived at my mother's to spend the night.

Wentie brought home a twelve-year-old girl to help me. I will call her Peggy (not her true identity). She was smart, quick, willing and capable. Yet she was still in the fourth grade at school, boasting how she helped to run several teachers out of the community. She felt that she knew everything that could be taught to her. She stayed with us for two weeks. We felt she might like a trip to see her family. Against Wentie's wishes, I gave her five dollars. I never saw her again. I did get a nasty note from her mother saying, "You send Peggy's clothes home or I'll sue you"!

Some of the city people who rented rooms or cottages for the summer had boats. There was one style, which the fishermen called cat boats. Those contraptions carried more sail than other boats.

One very bright morning, I believe it was in 1930, two lads left French Village in one of these boats to visit friends further inland. Their course was probably around Indian Point and up the shore to Schooner Cove. When a southwest wind hits St. Margaret's Bay, you need a sturdy boat under you for even the quiet coves can be turbulent. The older of the two lads must have had a great deal of experience in handling the craft.

The boys started for home in strong breeze, but when they reached Croucher's Island, the younger lad was landed on the shore. The other got safely home and told their folks where he had left the boy.

Wentie brought him, oh so wet, cold and shivering to the house. I gave him Bert's clothes to wear. Talk about a tight squeeze, but we made it. I rinsed his clothes, gave him lunch and warmed him by the kitchen stove. I'm sure he was just getting comfortable when his brother, accompanied by two other boys, came in. I don't know if there was another or not. I wanted to keep the boy until his clothes were completely dry, but his rescuers said no. Wentie offered to tow them to, and around, Indian Point, but they did not accept. After they left,

I watched them bounce around for awhile. Wentie said they'd make it, so I quit watching.

Chapter thirteen

One day late in 1930, Wentie came home with a fifteen-year-old boy. The "Dirty 30's" were already being felt in large families. Arnold Dauphinee was illiterate, good natured, always pleasant and was exceedingly strong for his age. He seemed to think chewing tobacco was all it took to make a man of him. I soon let him know that he couldn't chew tobacco in our house. Wentie chewed tobacco when I married him, and one dirty tub in my kitchen was plenty. Arnold willingly agreed.

He was accepted as a member of the family. We paid him eight dollars a month as salary. I wanted to teach him primary and elementary studies along with our own children. That was a foolhardy thought on my part.

When the weather was too inclement to be outside, he'd sit tapping his feet and, in an annoying rhythm, say "Diddle, diddle". I think Wentie often sought refuge in the stable to get away from it. Finally, Wentie set up a fishnet arrangement for Arnold to knit sheets of netting. At least he was quiet. He stayed with us three and one-half years.

One beautiful moonlight, much-too-warm evening in summer, the six of us sat on the embankment by the lighthouse, telling stories, joking and singing songs. Wentie said, "Arnold, you sing a song". He giggled and joked and asked us to sing "When the Works All Done This Fall". We had never heard it and asked, "Do you know it"? "Yes." "Well sing it, please do." It was a long song, and the young scamp sang every word of it.

Arnold went in the boat so often with Wentie that he learned to operate the motor. More wonderful that that, Wentie

The evenings were busy times too. Here you see Wentie knitting a dip-net.

allowed him to use the motorboat, but only when absolutely necessary.

I see in a small book of Wentie's that in 1931 a Captain Kenny built a schooner. I remember so many people marvelled at this piece of work, for Captain Kenny was then an old man and did the work himself. He and his sister were from the Eastern Shore of Nova Scotia, but she had met, and married, a man from French Village, where they lived.

The building of the schooner was done at Burchell's wharf. Wentie towed it to Hubley's wharf for further fitting on October 14, 1931.

Captain Kenny and a young man sailed that boat from the cove at French Village to Halifax without either chart or compass. They left several days after the final fitting was finished. I heard they arrived safely in Halifax for schooner registration.

As before mentioned, Wentie seemed to be chronically ill. In March of 1932, he weakened and fretted more than usual.

Mid March, I insisted that he see a doctor—all to no avail. Near the end of the month he couldn't get out of bed. I began treating a boil on his left leg.

On April 4 Arnold was sent to the home of a faithful friend at Boutilier's Point, to ask him where to find a phone to call a doctor. The man told him to go with him. They went to Black Point, where they contacted a doctor from Hubbards. Both came to the island with Arnold. The doctor gave me special instructions about carrying on treatments. Arnold returned each of the men to his respective contact place.

Life went on pleasantly with lessons as usual and Arnold was happier than ever. He did his work well; although Wentie insisted I make a daily round of inspection to be sure the animals were well fed and watered.

As the old folk used to say, one trouble never comes alone. It didn't in our case. The children got heavy colds. Poor little Bert's turned into croup. One night I really feared for his life.

Finally, on April 15, I was off my feet with the flu. Arnold had to bring oil, lamp and equipment to Wentie's bedside; to be made ready to be placed into the reflector. Arnold was proud—he really grew up that night. Wentie was very glad to have Arnold's help. The children and I took it all in our stride.

Wentie also worried whether Arnold would keep the hard-grease cup of the motor filled, so the bearings wouldn't burn out, so he had Arnold bring the cups, oil and gasoline to the bedside also.

Remember, Arnold was unable to read or write, but he was jolly and served us well, accepting our chastisement and compliments with a grin.

Wentie's condition continued to worsen. On April 18, we again sent for the doctor. This time he said that Wentie should go to hospital. Wentie refused to co-operate and stayed home, unable to straighten his leg as new outbreaks developed. The doctor was most disappointed and said, "I can't do any more for you here, and your wife has more than she can handle now".

I dared not use the old-fashioned poultices, only clear water made into Boric Acid solution. Changing every half-hour was permissible; his leg was almost cooked.

We were all so exhausted, he fell asleep. I, not wanting to disturb him, lay on the sofa in our room. I heard him thrashing around, hitting the bedding and lamenting. I said, "What is the matter"? He said, "I didn't know where you were. If anything happens to you, what will I do? Come over here; you may catch a cold." Poor man, what were his thoughts lying there so helpless? He had been in bed almost a month.

He was only up a few days, when his leg began to straighten. With the aid of a cane, he felt that he could go ashore–that would be a tonic for him. He, chubby Bert and Arnold went to French Village. I did not go to the shore to meet them when they returned, as was my custom.

We got lunch over and went to the orchard to look over some plans for a garden.

Bert came running, saying, "Dad, your motorboat is going adrift–half way to Indian Point".

What they did with that boat, or where they left it, is beyond me. Had Arnold been alone, perhaps it could have been considered carelessness, but Wentie? Never!

There was a light north breeze blowing. Luckily, the boys could row faster than the boat drifted. Wentie was too lame to do anything, but fret.

At eighteen years of age, Arnold began to enjoy the company of young people his age and got careless about coming home. He'd go off on a lark and we never knew when to expect him back. He was no longer dependable.

One day, he came in very casually. He said that he came to clean the hen houses, but he had bought himself a dress suit. Being such a short fellow, he always found trouser legs were too long and had to have them shortened. No-one ashore would shorten these pants. He asked me to do it. I, too, refused him. Wentie came in plaintively saying, "You might do it for the poor kid".

Arnold obviously thought I wouldn't refuse him and quickly

produced the pants. When they were shortened, I told him the job was done. He asked me how much he owed. I knew he didn't have a nickel to his name, so I said, "Arnold, it will take you the rest of your life to pay me for this job". He gave me a strange look. I said, "I want you to straighten up and forget the rowdy habits that you have recently developed. You are a strong boy and can earn a good living with a clean character. He gave me a broad grin and said, "I'll do dat".

According to Wentie's records, Arnold was between the island and the mainland until May. It was only a few weeks, when we heard that Arnold was in trouble again and was placed in detention, where he and his companion caught a germ in their throats. His friend, with good home care, recovered. Arnold did not survive. His body rests in St. Margaret's Cemetery in Tantallon.

In April, 1932, we received the sad news that Grace and Hiram lost their infant son at birth on April 26. Grace had a difficult time and was several months recovering.

I can't recall everyday details, but I know a calf was born on the island during 1932. It was a male. At first Arnold played with it, then teased it, causing it to become cross. When it was a year old, it was castrated, but was still too mean to break in for work. He had a mean disposition and nobody wanted him. The only thing that frightened him was an Irish Terrier dog, Rex, which was our family pet. After awhile, Rex also turned mean, but not with us—just visitors.

Three mainlanders were working together in the beef business. They knew Ginger, the bull, was bad even though he had been neutered. However, they still thought that he should bring a good price.

I guess they had an exciting time getting him ashore and onto a truck. They kept him on it all night. The next morning, he was fastened to a ringbolt and taken from the truck. I understand that butchering job proved to be an interesting one as well. However, after Ginger was marketed, we were given a very small sum of money as the meat was classed as bull meat.

Though he had never serviced another animal, he was to old when doctored.

One night, when Russell (Wentie's nephew, who came to live with us after Arnold left) went to stable Ginger, he laid his hand on the bull's rump. Ginger wheeled and Russell went down in a second. Bert saw what happened and came for the dog, Rex, but the bull had already gored through a new pair of overalls and pants. Russell was free of any physical harm, but quite unnerved, as we all were.

The darned thing even put me over the woodpile one day. Once again, Rex was the hero. All that expense, worry and adventure for nothing but exercise.

By now the depression crunch was hitting people hard. Wentie was buying a pound of lard or tea, matches or soap for adults and treats for small children, who stood at his elbow when shopping. He would come home and tell me of some poor soul who had no mittens, or can you spare a pair of socks for such-and-such a person.

He was always willing to carry gifts of homemade cookies or flowers to a sick friend. His mother would often say to him, "So-and-so would like to have some of Maggie's molasses cookies, doughnuts or jelly". Those were the specialties.

One mistake that I could not make was to dress a pail in pretty paper. "You remember the saying, 'the eye is half of the appetite'?" Oh, oh, no delivery! "Tear it off!" Though Wentie was forever carrying some goodies to someone, he never wanted undue attention drawn to the fact. If a parcel was wrapped to fancy, then it stayed home.

As for a knitted gift for someone, that meant nothing to me. I had been brought up in a large family. Mum and Dad's business was lumbering and mixed farming with sheep for wool and food. I knew a lot about knitting wool, but could not spin. Nor did I know how much raw wool was required to spin a pound of yarn, nor the quantity required for a pair of mitts or socks. The amount of yarn on hand was endless from one year's end to the next; just keep knitting. On the island,

I'd learn how to spin. "By dewey", as old-time mail-driver Charlie Mahar used to say, I'll order four pounds of wool from Grace.

She said, "What in the world will Maggie do with four pounds of wool'? Lester said, "Knit a mitten for the island"! Mum gave me her spinning wheel. It was time-consuming, but a pleasant pastime and, joy of joys, I learned to spin and had oodles of yarn. For the time being, it was white or gray, cuddly warm and cost only $1.00 per pound. The store-bought yarn was nineteen cents an ounce.

Wentie bought dye. The colours were pretty. I could not understand knitting instructions, but I knitted snowsuits, mittens, bonnets, socks, petticoats and slippers with pure wool inside. I just had to learn how to read instructions, which I mastered after awhile.

Before I could "knit a mitten for the island", the wool had to be spun into yarn.

Chapter fourteen

A Mr. Fredericks owned Indian Point. To be more explicit, he owned a large portion of Indian Point. He and his wife had a large family. They all married, with the exception of one boy, who suffered from a disability throughout his life.

Mrs. Fredericks and a daughter passed away in early 1919 due to aftereffects of the 1918 flu, which ravaged the whole continent. A widowed daughter with several children came to keep the home together. When her children were old enough to look for work and her girls got married, she also went out to earn her way,

Mr. Fredericks and his son had no source of income. They had been selling the fishing gear, animals and farm machinery. When it was all gone, Mr. Fredericks gave his home to a married son, who lived in Bedford and was employed at various jobs, including freight handling at the Halifax Waterfront and in Montreal. He and his wife also had a large family.

On August 29, 1934, he and a group of his relatives from Head of St. Margaret's Bay came to the island. They stayed for dinner and he spent the night at our house.

Next morning, Wentie and young Mr. Fredericks went out and returned within the hour. They announced that Wentie had bought the old homestead at Indian Point. Like it or lump it, there it was! Why not?

Buying the property meant new repairs on the house; paint, torn-down chimneys to repair, etc. It was pretty when finished, but Wentie and his brother, Doss, never could repair all the leaks. New tools had to be bought. It was a nuisance carrying, often forgetting, something urgently needed either at the Point or on the island. It was amazing to see how badly things were needed outside for barns, boats and fishing gear. Teams were hired, more often loaned, for ploughing and hay making.

The children and I took it in our stride, but it was a drain on our purse strings. During the winter, Wentie's trips to the mainland paid off. He was advised to run up another hen house to help meet finances and, best of all, to keep everybody busy—"Eat no idle bread in our house"! So up went a pig shed and another henhouse. We now had a barn, brooder and two houses, in addition to the above-mentioned buildings. Alas, now Wentie also needed a new heated workshop, so he could build boats. We could concentrate on this, because Mr. Fredericks had leased the old homestead to a family whom, early in the game, found that it requires more than a hoe and a rake to be a farmer, but, of course, we were not aware of this when we bought the farm.

The lessee knew a city dweller, a talkative, willing worker who would operate the farm. Nobody could work on an empty stomach, without tools and support a wife and child. The farm deal fell through, which was a blow dealt to many during the "Dirty 30's".

Wentie entered the picture at this point. We allowed Ed, the would-be farmer, to live there rent-free. Wentie occasionally brought them a few food staples. Wentie was kind to many in those days.

In the summer of 1935 or 1936, Ed got a job as a carpenter at one dollar a day. He had to walk about four miles to his work and back again at night. Soon he acquired a skeleton of a bicycle and he was in the money. He felt like a millionaire, while Wentie felt like an abused benefactor. After all that he had done for Ed, Ed left just when he was most needed for haying. Poor Ed, I guess he did the best that he could.

Meanwhile, I had become pregnant. Wentie did not receive the news well. In my girlhood home such news would be accepted joyously, but nowhere in the family into which I had married was pregnancy eagerly looked forward to by any member of the family, be it their concern or not.

So in 1933-34, I learned the meaning and anguish of mental cruelty. Ethel would say, "Mother, you do not sing anymore". "We Live In Two Different Worlds, Dear, That's Why We're So Far Apart" would go through my mind. As I nightly said my prayers, I held an imaginary picture of my dear deceased father before me and prayed my precious child would be as noble and good as my beloved parent had been.

In the spring, I thought I'd go away for awhile. We had an old trunk. Wentie carefully took it apart, reserving the iron parts and outer decorations. He made a new trunk, tray and all. We placed it on the kitchen table and covered the outer part with canvas using a large pot of homemade glue. He then painted it gray, doing the iron parts in black or brass, as he deemed proper. I covered the inside with wallpaper. The work really was a credit to each of us. As things turned out, I didn't use the trunk after all. Time passed happily for us in the lighthouse. We bought only a few hens that spring.

The time came for me to leave. Once again Wentie was negotiating with his family to bring home a nephew of his, who was orphaned in 1921 and had spent a number of years in a boys' home in Colchester County, Nova Scotia. Of course, he couldn't bring him to the island, while Maggie would be away. Cliff had the answer to that. "Bring him to my house". Fine. Settled.

I was to leave home May 24 and stay with Wentie's sister in Halifax. My baby was due on May 28. On that day, all of Canada was agog with the arrival of the Dionne quintuplets. My children had heavy colds in May. Poor Bert had such terribly painful earache with his. Our girls were quite capable of taking care of things at home, but Wentie must have someone else to stay with them.

I had several trips in to the Grace Maternity Hospital, each time being sent out with a warning not to leave the city. I did leave. I came to my mother's house in Tantallon. I was there ten days, when I finally realized that I was not in false labour, but was having the real thing.

My brother took me in to the hospital at 6:00 a.m. Our little son, Wayne Dalton, was ushered into the world June 29, 1934, as Mr. Norman Hubley, Seabright, made his demise on his seventy-ninth birthday. How we all loved our blue-eyed darling baby.

Wentie came to take Wayne and me to the lighthouse. I wanted to have the baby baptized first. Wentie had a cold and wouldn't go to church with me. His sister stood with me. The Church Organist of St. Paul's stayed to play a hymn, but the Minister didn't announce one.

Wayne and I were not to leave the island from September until April, a period of seven months. We then went, because he was very ill. We had to get him to a doctor.

It was Easter Monday. Wentie said, "I'll take you and baby to your Mother's". My brother had a car, but was not at home. Wentie's brother, Dawson, of French Village, had a car, but he was building a store for a Mr. Mason at Head of St. Margaret's Bay. He couldn't afford to lose a day's pay, but offered to let his car go, if we could find a driver.

Mr. Mason said his brother could drive the car. He did bring the car to my mother's; my brother came home while we were getting ready. Mr. Mason asked my brother to drive Dawson's car, because he (Mr. Mason) had a nasty headache. It seemed that he was subject to frequent headaches.

Mr. Mason sat in the back seat, while Wayne and I were made comfortable in the front seat. There was no pavement between Tantallon and Halifax. The roads were bad all over due to spring thaw, but were nearly impassable in the coloured settlement of Beechville; clear old gumbo right up to the running boards (a piece of equipment no longer installed in cars today).

Half a dozen Negroes said, "Hold it White, hold it!", but my brother kept trying to move on and got stuck. My brother said, "C'mon, boys, give me a push". They just stood there grinning. Mr. Mason jumped out of the car and said, "Come on boys, there is a sick baby in this car who urgently needs a doctor".

Those fine coloured men jumped in unison. I'm sure there were enough of them to carry car, and all, through the mire. Bless their hearts, we were soon on our way again. I had learned that black people are warm, kind-hearted individuals if treated graciously.

When we reached Halifax, I didn't know where to go, so I chose the doctor that got the credit for delivering the baby. Neither the doctor nor I recognized each other, but he gave me an admittance paper to take Wayne to the hospital. I was still nursing Wayne and didn't want to leave him. We went up to Wentie's sister's house. Wentie's mother was there and gave a negative opinion about the hospital plan. His niece was secretary to a number of doctors and suggested I take Wayne to a child's doctor. "Who'? "We are not allowed to choose, only suggest. Our family has always been treated by Dr. Carney".

We took Wayne to see him. The doctor said, "I don't know who told you to take your baby to a hospital, but I'm telling you to take him home with you. Here is a prescription for medication and a paper that will get you to a hospital, if need be, without seeing another doctor". We came home and Wayne was fine for two years.

The summer Wayne was born, I did not go to the hayfield. The men had to come home for dinner. The girls went to the field with them in the afternoon. On the last haymaking day in August of that year, 1934, they finished at dusk, which left me with all the chores to do at home. Why not? I was accustomed to it.

Russell was Wentie's nephew. He would be treated just like a member of the family and would work without any pay. He understood from the supervisor at the home that he was being hired. Somehow that didn't show up in Wentie's and Cliff's books. Russell was a stalwart, quiet, almost morose person. How he loved our baby Wayne. He stayed with us over three years. Before he left us, he was confirmed with our girls in St. Paul's Church, French Village. He left on November 1, 1938, and joined the army when the hostilities of World War II broke out, September 3, 1939.

He later married a girl from Kings County, N.S., Edith Robertson. Their first, and only, son was named Wayne Dalton. They later had two girls, Shirley and Linda. They bought a home in West Glenmont. Edith was again pregnant. She worked too hard improving the home. Complications set in and Edith died in childbirth. Russell would not allow the baby out of his care. Unfortunately, it too died. It was only five months of age.

Misfortune was not new to Russell. When his son, Wayne, was three years old, he and a group of children were burning garbage in the backyard. Wayne fell into the fire. He spent three years in the hospital recovering from those third-degree burns. Both his mother and father gave skin grafts, but his father's grafts did not take. He was such a pathetic looking darling, although his face was not scarred.

Russell was in the army, when Wayne was burned so seriously. Dear little Wayne's first doctor was not familiar with burn treatments. Russell went to the army doctor, who was the base hospital doctor. Russell recognized him as being the doctor that had treated our Wayne in the lighthouse. The doctor ordered the burnt child to the Children's Hospital in Halifax.

After Russell lost the baby, he moved to British Columbia. I talked to him and his family from Alberta in 1981. His son, Wayne, is married and has two sons. The oldest one is Wayne Dalton. How do we separate the three of them?

I do not know where Russell was on the night of August 15, 1935. It was such a beautiful night and oh, so hot! Wentie and the children were asleep as I cleaned vegetables by the light of the moon, to cook for dinner at the hayfield the next day. Many friends and relatives came for haying, making a picnic out of it. Wentie, Bert and Russell would go early in the

Making hay is a lot of hard work, so everyone pitches in.

morning; the girls and I would cook dinner to serve hot in the hayfield. We had to row over a mile and a quarter and back again, to and from the hayfield on Indian Point. If we were lucky, we got away before the wind came in! Only once did Wentie have to come after us with the motorboat.

After I had finished the vegetables at midnight, I cleared things up and went to bed. In a light doze I heard a pounding on the door. How unusual. I hurriedly slipped into a house-coat and ran to the door to see and hear a young woman dressed in white, carrying a large pole and crying, "Oh God, there's nobody here". I called, "Wait a minute'! She turned. By then Wentie was out to see what was happening. The lady told us that she was rooming at the Seabright Hotel, which was owned and operated by a Mr. Hubley and was situated on the shore of one of the many coves in St. Margaret's Bay. It's a delightful place to see, either from the land or sea. Visitors enjoyed boating during their stay and had all been told that if they lost their bearings to follow the cry of the seagulls, because a small island near the mouth of Hubley's Cove had nothing on it but seagulls. The cove was so secluded that the trees cast a dark

shadow over all.

The above-mentioned young couple hired a boat for the evening. It was such a beautiful night that none could blame them for drifting and dreaming with no thought of time. The hotel proprietor didn't explain that seagulls also fish by night in fishermen's nets, and the young couple saw their error much too late. Panic took over. Not looking, they just rowed to catch a gull. God was surely merciful that night to let the water be calm and with only a low surf running.

Finally, in desperation, they headed for our light. The man stayed with the boat while the girl, using the pole, inched her way up the perpendicular bank of our island. It's a miracle they could even maneuver their way in over those treacherous rocks. The tide was so very low.

Wentie said to me, "You guide this lady down our path. When you hear my motorboat coming, get them both into their boat and tell him to row to meet me. When you hear me coming home, come meet me".

She and I got down on the shore, where precious few people ever ventured. He was a gentleman and didn't want me, a mere woman, to shove him out on the Bay. The lady said, "Do what she says, Art"! Few people questioned Wentie's orders, so I got them far enough out that Wentie was able to take them aboard and tow their heavy old fishing boat back to the cove. They reached the hotel. Only the girl, Laura, was staying there. Art was at a private dwelling in Glen Margaret and wanted to be taken there. Wentie was not familiar with that area and was afraid for his boat. To hit a rock at high speed could be disastrous, but he risked it and took the chap home.

I did not know what was taking place, but waited. When I heard the motor growing fainter, I surmised someone was off course. Should I wait for him or say farewell, Sailor Boy, and return to bed. After all, I had been up all night anyway. I did wait. It was almost daybreak when we got the boats put away and got back to the lighthouse.

They returned the following Sunday with the young lady's father to properly thank Wentie for his trouble. Russell was at home alone. It so happened that it was just one of those days some of our relatives chose to take our family on a trip. The trips our relatives took us on often proved most educational for the children and helped them greatly in their Correspondence Study Courses.

Wentie never reported a rescue or tow to the Government or even made a charge for a kind deed. All was done through the goodness of this heart, bless him. Wentie was telling somebody about it afterward. He said he didn't rush out because he thought it might be someone coming to rob us. Of what, I wondered. We had nothing worth taking. He thought I wasn't using my head—rushing out like that!

Chapter fifteen

Grace and Hiram didn't think of the summer being complete without a few trips to the island. Friends came from hither and yon. One group was a Halifax merchant's family, though he did not accompany them as he was too lame. Though the group varied, many returned several times.

Often the weather would turn dull, the sea kick up a chop, and folks would be detained longer than intended. On one such day, Grace and Hiram were headed for the island. Hiram was a tease and had a most vivid imagination. He told one lady that when a storm was brewing, Wentie would have to put out anchors all around the island to keep it from going adrift. Land sakes!

On the day that Grace and Hiram arrived, the men were slinging their anchors to set the seine. Hiram says, " Wentie, you expecting a storm?" Wentie replied, "Yes", feeling sure Hiram was kidding somebody. That poor woman was uneasy.

Sure enough, in the afternoon, one of those sneaky little summer storms came up. It was chilly and quite lengthy. Now that poor woman was terrifed. It took quite a bit of talking to convince her that the island could not actually drift away.

We never worried much about getting a meal on the table. I usually had canned meat, but folks preferred fresh fish, when we could get it. Plenty of eggs, milk, butter, pickles and jams, with quick breads of various sorts.

We had had dinner while the sun shone; but by supper it was another matter, with a cold rain falling. I fretted–I don't know what to get. Grace said, "pancakes"! She made them, while I fried up potatoes (in those days, a meal wasn't a meal

Now where am I supposed to find a pot big enough to cook this?

without potatoes). We set up blocks of wood with boards on them for seats, and we were well away. The table was large enough for all.

Wentie had just brought home a five-pound can of corn syrup a few days' earlier.

He had paid a mere thirty-five cents for it. We opened it, and I put a big iron mixing spoon into the can; everybody was happily eating. A lad, about thirteen years old, asked to have the syrup passed to him. Hiram (drat him) said "Don't eat too much of that. It costs money". The boy sat there, spoon in midair, aghast! I, too, was initially shocked and said, "Hiram, how could you"?! A twinkle shone in Hiram's eye. Everybody laughed heartily and proceeded to eat, but you didn't know what to expect from Hiram next. The weather cleared and the folks were able to travel home in a colourful sunset.

Schoolchildren were brought to the island for Arbour Day Picnics, usually on the first Friday in May. Sometimes Wentie would bring Girl Guides for a boat ride. Grace and Hiram would come at butchering time, and the chicken business was proceeding on, as usual.

People knew that I had two girls, who should be able to do a lot of work. Some thought they were doing us a favour by offering to keep them for household chores. Ethel worked for a short while for a minister, also a summer season at a hotel and then with my mother for awhile. She eventually married Harold Kennedy of Boutilier's Point. Dean worked a short while for Mother, until Wentie decided that she should come home.

The winter I was pregnant with Wayne, Wentie was anything but happy about the whole thing. My later pregnancy with Joyce aroused none of the same animosity. It was obviously a reaction caused by war nerves that made him so unpleasant that one winter.

When Joyce was born at the Halifax Infirmary on August 9, 1936, our girls kept house. Wentie was well away–he had Russell. Wentie's uncles were down from the U.S.A. One, an old sea captain, was high in his praise for our girls.

When I came home with Joyce, I wanted Grace to come to church with me to have the baby baptized. Grace was sick in bed with pneumonia. Joyce was our only child taken to the island before she was baptized. Her baptism finally took place on October 17, 1937, without witnesses in attendance..

Chapter sixteen

The sea is beautiful to gaze upon; pleasant to be on sometimes, but in a raging storm not even rocks can withstand its
fury. Land is washed away; rocks are ground into sand. So it
was with Indian Point; a large portion of it washed away leaving a sand beach between Indian Point proper, the Nubic and
what is now called Micou's island. The latter was owned by a
Mr. Boutilier, who sold it in the early 1930's to an American
lawyer, a Mr. Micou from New York, U.S.A. The only way to
reach the island now is by boat at high tide or by walking the
beach at low tide.

I may mention here how much the Micou's enjoyed this
home through the intervening years until 1945, when Mr.
Micou had a dental problem. He didn't recover, and his cre-
mated remains rest on the Nubic. The surviving Micou family
retained the home and came visiting each summer. They missed
several summers during the war years. Sometimes the house
was leased to Halifax people for a few months.

People could not get beyond the gate of our land on Indian Point with their cars. Mr. Micou bought a small plot of
land from Henry Dauphinee for a place to build a shelter for
his car. During a storm the wind lifted the garage over a fence
and flattened it on our well–a distance of approximately thirty
feet.

The Micou's had friends who wished to summer in Nova
Scotia near the Micou family. Our house on Indian Point
seemed to be quite satisfactory. The Machlett family (of Ger-
man descent) was from Stamford, Conneticutt, U.S.A. and

consisted of Mr. and Mrs. Machlett, one son, two daughters and a maid, Olga. They were fine people.

Every ten days or two weeks they had a new group of friends visiting them. We met many Americans each summer, some of whom were descendants of William Harkness, owner of the yacht, *Gunilda*, which Wentie sailed on when it was ship-wrecked on Lake Superior.

The Machlett's hired Dawson Boutilier's boat, *The Madcap*, sail and motor combined. Daily matter-of-fact things to us interested and intrigued those people so much. We were amused at the little things, which gave them so much pleasure.

One day Wentie showed Mr. Machlett and his son a sea egg; a curse in fishing gear and lobster pots. They had to have the whole story–where to get them, how, etc. They spent two days diving and playing with sea eggs and sand dollars.

I don't know if Mr. Machlett spent too much time under-water or if he had it coming from another source, but the poor man got an earache. It was very painful and lasted for days. He was admitted to hospital. So I wrote:

Sand dollars are thick on the shores of the Bay
Where the Machlett's come each summer to play
Mr. Machlett went diving among them in fun
But go a sore ear which made him run
To a Halifax doctor, yelling with pain
The doctor said, "Don't go diving again"
Oh how his ear ached, it felt like hot lead
Poor man couldn't stand on his feet or his head
'Til relief came; it broke in the night
Which made us all happy–our hearts grew light
But the doctor said "Put your hands in your jeans
My boy, we want pay, and NEVER AGAIN
DIVE INTO THAT BAY!"
For razor, sand dollar, a mussel or clam
The old-fashioned dollar is best by a DAMN.

The Machlett's had a five-year lease, which they held and paid for even though they only used it two summers. War broke out in 1939, which made a difference in the lives of many people. I wrote several more verses about their children, but I forget them and did not keep copies.

The rental to the Machlett's meant we had a lot of work to do. We put the garden in and repaired and cleaned the house. Our own girls had to do the housework on the island, while I did the work on the Point. Sometimes Wentie came with Russell and me to work, but since he had done the inside painting during the winter months the rest of the inside work was up to me, while Russell worked outside.

One dull day Russell and I were heading home about 4:30 p.m. We were both rowing the boat when a very large yacht, rigged for albacore fishing, eased around the southern end of the island. A big man, grinning like a Cheshire cat, stood in the pulpit. The boat kept getting nearer and nearer, while the man's grin got wider and wider. As it got dangerously near and kept bearing down, Russell exclaimed, "Pull, Aunt Maggie, PULL–FOR GOD'S SAKE–PULL. They are going to run us down". As the big thing loomed over us, we could see emblazoned on the bow in black and gold letters "Marblehead, Mass., U.S.A." At the last second, as a collision seemed inevitable, he put his helm over and hove-to alongside our boat. He asked us if we had seen any tuna. I felt like telling him that all I had seen recently was a grinning fool and his yacht, but I held my tongue. It was a chartered vessel with a local fisherman from Lunenburg as skipper, who felt he was taking a rise out of us, while the American enjoyed our oarsmanship. They called it a joke. We just called it stupid.

Mr. Machlett developed a terminal illness and died quite young. Mrs. Machlett resumed teaching, while the eldest girl remained a spinster and went into medicine. I heard their son and youngest daughter married young; however, they both married.

While we were making hay on the Point in 1937-38, Wayne

had a recurrence of his former illness. No-one explained to me what it was, but I've seen enough suffering since then to call it urine retention.

I didn't realize when I started to write that I could remember so many incidents. This particular one developed on Saturday and we had just returned from haymaking to the island. The moon shone down in glory upon us, while a strong northwest wind blew. Wayne needed my full attention. I had no idea what caused his sickness or where his pain, if any, was located.

About midnight I said to Wentie, "You've got to get me a doctor for this child". There weren't any local doctors nearby, but there were a number of summer visitors with no desire to practice while on holidays.

Wentie said, "I don't know what to do or where to go". I suggested several doctors whom he might try. He didn't approve of any one of them, but he said, "Get Russell out"!

I aroused Russell and they set out. I don't remember where all they went, because Wentie didn't want to disturb householders. A Dr. Campbell, veteran of World War One, was living permanently in Seabright. Wentie saw a light there so he inquired, but Dr. Campbell was on duty in Halifax. Mrs. Campbell was a nurse and offered to come to the island. She took Wayne's temperature–104 degrees. She left some pills, with directions for use, saying "Don't be afraid, they won't do any harm and may help. Poor little fellow".

Wentie took Mrs. Campbell back home and she asked Wentie to wait until she phoned her husband. Dr. Campbell said, "If you have a child with a temperature of 104 degrees, you have a much too sick child, and I cannot get there until tomorrow."

Before Wentie returned home again, Wayne was able to urinate. His temperature soon began to go down. The next day Wentie brought Dr. Campbell to the island, where he did a slight operation on Wayne. We never had a repeat of that illness.

I believe it was prior to the above illness that Wayne had broken his arm. Wentie thought that it was just a bruise. I said, "Take me to a doctor with this child". "Oh, alright–get ready!"

We took him to a Kennedy home in Boutilier's Point, where Wentie went to phone for a doctor. We caught the doctor treating a patient bedridden with pneumonia in Tantallon.

When the doctor saw Wayne, he diagnosed his arm as broken; a green-stick fracture, bent on one side and split. Mr. Kennedy helped Wentie to look for a shingle, from which they shaved a splint.

Wentie announced that he would go visiting, as he liked doctors far apart and few between. While he was gone, Wayne was put asleep and the arm was set. He was restless for a few days, but the arm healed well.

Wayne had broken his arm on April 24, 1937. On September 16, 1938, he started to get pains in his side that would draw his right leg up. On this particular day, Wentie said, "We will take him to a doctor".

Wentie took us to Boutilier's Point and ran to find someone with a vehicle to take Wayne and me to Halifax. The best we could find was a man with a four-ton truck. He took us up the Bay somewhere. Then he found our son-in-law, Harold Kennedy, who was doing some carpenter work. The men exchanged truck for car, and away we went, once again to our good friend, Dr. Carney.

After careful examination, the good doctor said, "Your son has a bad case of pin worms, which have infected the appendix". I said, "that means a treatment of Quassa Chips". The doctor said, "No! go to the seashore and get a pint of seawater; heat it to body temperature and give him an enema of the solution once a day for a week. If he gets restless after that, repeat the instruction". I had to repeat it just once more. I can tell you that with our family record of appendix operations, it sure gave us a heck of a scare.

I cannot find a note that refers to Wayne's earache, but he

had one. No home remedy that I knew about could relieve his pain. We had Dr. Homans to him twice, yet no relief. The dear little fellow would beat his head against the wall. Once again we sent for the doctor, but he refused to come, saying there was nothing he could do and that we should take the child to hospital. On his second visit, I had suggested syringing the ear. Dr. Homans would not give consent to this method.

With our small child suffering so, I thought, 'Fi, fi, doctor; yes or no, here goes for syringing'. I knew it was dangerous in my inexperienced hands, but nothing could be worse than standing by watching my little tot's suffering. A new drug was on the market, which was known as Hygeol. I made up a solution, wrapped a few towels around his little neck and, with a prayer in my heart and one on my lips, I exhausted the air from a tiny rectum syringe, the only one I had. I filled it with Hygeol solution, slowly and gently inserted it into the ear, squeezed the syringe and then slowly withdrew it from the child's ear. I repeated the procedure twice more. At last–relief! I used the same treatment for a few more days. I've never known Wayne to have ear trouble since.

When I had Wayne to the doctor for his pinworms, I told the doctor of the experience. Strangely enough he said, "You and the doctor were both right. The tract needed cleansing, but there was danger of flushing the infection into the mastoid gland and then there really would have been trouble". More often than not, our home remedies were as much good judgement as good medicine.

Chapter seventeen

Fishing in the Bay in 1938 was labour in vain. All work and not enough fish for the table. One morning in September I asked Bertram to row over to Indian Point, where a fisherman had his seine set. On his arrival at the seine Bert said, "can we get a mess of fish for dinner?" the man replied, "My boy, there is just one fish in there. If you can get it, you can have it'!

The fish was a monstrous shark. It required a pair of oxen to haul just the head away. The pesky thing enveloped itself so badly in the gear that it drowned itself, but not before it completely ruined the seine. That was a terrible loss.

On January 20, 1939, we stood in our kitchen window and watched the burning of a hotel at Queensland, Halifax County, Nova Scotia. The hotel was owned and operated by a Mr. and Mrs. Dorey. Many members of their own family were on staff.

A Halifax jeweller had a summer cottage built on the ground. He hired Bert to excavate under it in Bert's spare time, for he was very interested in Bert and found his manner pleasing. He was knowledgeable and willing to work. Their friendship was mutual, each accepting the work as time permitted. So Bert drudged at home and earned a few dollars working on the mainland when time permitted. Hence, Bertram started out with a good character reference.

He wanted things so dear to a young boy's heart. He was always interested in airplanes, so I got him a book with twenty-five cents and a couple of baking powder coupons. With his first earned money, he bought two books for eight dollars. His father was displeased. Dad didn't like airplanes.

Next, Bert bought a Charles Atlas course and bit of equipment, then a guitar. While I thought that he was being quite sensible, the other side of the house said, "Oh, oh; naughty, naughty."

When he was sixteen-and-a-half years old, he found employment that took him away from home. When he told his father that he was going, Dad was stunned. I was in the garden when Wentie came to me, troubled. I returned to the house closely followed by my dear husband. He made a statement that I did not like. I faced him and quietly said, "I admire Bert's ambition–he has every right to go"! Poor Dad, he never dreamed I'd oppose him. When Bert reached eighteen, he joined the Royal Canadian Air Force.

When Bert and Dean were still at home, I used to get deathly headaches. One morning I awoke with one of my headaches. Oh, I was so sick. Dean was doing housework on the mainland for one month for a family of five, where a new baby was expected. Dad said, "I'm going to send Bert for Dean". I said, "Not with my say so". Dad said, "Bert, go for Dean". Bert went, but the new baby had arrived the previous night and Dean loyally refused to come. I was proud of her.

Poor Wentie lamented badly; he felt alone. There were so many on the mainland to take care of each other, but no-one to help him. I sufficiently recovered by noon to handle our own affairs. Wentie was quiet, but extremely nervous.

On September 15, 1940, Ethel and I went ashore. Wentie thought he was the only one who knew how to tie a boat. The truth is he didn't want us to go ashore, but we went anyway. On our return home, I tied the boat myself.

A storm raged Sunday night, all day and all Monday night. No-one had any thought or fear of damage to the boats. Tuesday morning Bert went to the shore. The destruction was unbelievable. The motorboat was off the ramp with her side stove in. The dinghy was completely gone. The flat had one foot of its nose tied to the boathouse exactly as I had tied it, the rest of the boat bashed its way along the shore until it found a clear spot in the woods to hide.

Bert was so excited, he rushed to the house to tell the news. Wentie was more sick from hearing about it than the work required to repair his badly needed boats.

Wentie, Bert, Ethel and I picked up our poor boat and carried it down overland and put it into the boathouse. Ethel went to the house. Wentie said "I'll work on the boat, you and Bert clean the launchway."

The launchway was so full of rocks that we didn't know where to look for it. The rocks were so huge that we should have had oxen to pull them out. Bert and I worked two days and still didn't get it all done.

Wentie worked equally as hard trying to make the boat tight, but he might as well have tried to mend a basket. They put the boat in the water, but could not bail as fast as it filled. We were stranded without a boat. Dean was away at the time visiting on Ironbound island.

One of Wentie's nephews who lived in Queens County always came to see us when visiting the area. He used Cliff's boat to come to the island, then he and Wentie went to Boutilier's Point. A Mr. Awalt loaned us his boat for the winter. Wentie had to tow our boat to a boat-builder in Seabright for repairs. Wentie mended the dinghy himself after we found it.

Wentie continued to complain of his chronic condition, so Bert returned home for the winter of 1941-42. Wentie was unwell, though not bedridden, for the month of December.

One dark, bleak morning of the week between Christmas and New Years, he said, "Take me ashore. I have to go to a doctor. Come meet me tonight for I may be able to come home". He could scarcely move as he went to the boat. Bert took him to Boutilier's Point, where someone took him to a doctor. Dr. Little diagnosed his case as shingles, which, in itself, is a painful condition, but he was also sick with his war nerves.

The doctor said it was a crime that he was demobilized from the army without a pension. However, Wentie returned home in a happy frame of mind with his weeping blisters all bandaged. Now that he knew what it was, he could cope with it. He later told folks that he was scared to let me know what his condition was, because I'd make him go to a doctor. Oh, be Gorrah!

Wayne was very much attached to his Dad and spent a lot of time with him. One night when preparing Wayne for bed, he complained of an itch. I stripped him off and found ten blisters scattered over him. I called Wentie to see. He said, "Oh-h-h, do you think he got the same damn stuff I got'? Next morning a few more blisters were there. I said, "Dad, come see; this child has chicken pox". In a worried tone he said, "I don't know.

We had Ethel's oldest child, our first grandchild, at the house. I was bathing her and up pops a blister! On examination Joyce showed a dozen more blisters. Dean and Bert had so many that I'd describe it as only one blister, they were so completely covered. It was hateful, cleaning and tending them, trying unsuccessfully to alleviate the itching. Those two were really sick for a few days. We didn't have a doctor in, and I was the only one able to do housework, stable work and tend the light. Meanwhile, Dean was to go to work for Ethel, who was in the Halifax Infirmary with her second daughter.

A terrible storm came up about January 29. Another woman on Kennedy Point was in childbirth labour. A group of men made a stretcher, carried her to a truck and took her to hospital. Wentie said to me, "If you can get a little milk from the cow for the sake of the children, let the hens go. Let the eggs freeze." It was no harder to care for the hens than for the cow and to get water into the house, so I had a party even though Wentie and the children fretted.

Next morning the world was so beautiful. Every tree, fence, building, the whole earth covered with glistening white snow as the sun shone from a cloudless sky. The wind was something else. As I put out the light, the tower trembled. I dressed to do the outdoor chores. The snow was waist deep as I trundled my way with milk pail, shoulder high, carrying a bucket of water in two hands before me to water the hens. When I returned from the stable and hen house, the same picture was presented to view for the northwest wind blew so hard that not a track was visible anywhere.

When Dean got better, she went to Ethel's for a few weeks. Spring soon came and everyone was feeling better. Bert went away again.

About this time, ships began to convoy in the Bay. Wentie began to watch and register the names and hull numbers of the various styles of ships: destroyers, steamers, frigates, corvettes, fairmiles and q-boats that came into the Bay.

One ship, the *Acadia*, known as the doctor's ship, laid up at the northeast corner of an island commonly known among the fishermen as Willie Harry's island. Another large steamer, the *St. Clair*, lay at a buoy midway between our island and Indian Point. We were advised that it was American owned, unfit for overseas transport and was on loan to Canada. She was being used as a supply ship.

There was also some training done in St. Margaret's Bay. When we no longer saw familiar ships come in, it meant they had become part of a convoy and were enroute overseas.

The crew members were not usually, in fact not at all, allowed shore leave, but of an evening, the lads would slip to the lighthouse for a game of cards or Chinese checkers.

One night there was an unusually bad chimney fire in the lighthouse. An order went out to all ships, stand by for service and rescue work at the lighthouse. Fortunately, we didn't need assistance.

I can only remember two chimney fires while living there and one was earlier than the aforementioned one. Wentie was away, as he so often was. Joyce was only a few months old. As the older children and I watched the flames leaping so high in the air, it was eleven-year-old Bert who had the presence of mind to say "Mother, I'm going in to bring the baby out". All was well when Wentie arrived home.

In the early 1940's, a submarine was grounded on a reef above Clam island and was towed to safety by either a frigate or corvette.

One seagoing ship was carrying a contingent of airmen, six of whom were given overnight shore leave. Those stalwart men were looking for the shortest route to Hubbards, where dances were held. They made the mistake of coming south of Wood island, where lies an unmarked reef. The surf carried them in and capsized their boat.

Wentie went over and assisted in recovering thole-pins, oars and uprighting the boat. He invited them to our humble home to get dried out. They declined the invitation, wrung out their clothes, emptied the water from their shoes and returned to the ship; foregoing the happy anticipation of song, dance and genial association with the public in general.

One very dark night, Wentie and Dean were at Oliver Dauphinee's in Boutilier's Point. He owned a merchant store and was the postmaster. I had put the two small children to bed and was sewing. A knock came on the door–unusual at that time of night. I did not take a light as I answered the door (the main door to the lighthouse was closed in autumn and not opened again until May; therefore, the only entrance was through the woodshed to the kitchen for genteel and humble alike).

As I stood there, three large men faced me. They were polite and asked if they could buy some milk. The dog was not satisfied and raised fury. I said, "What have you got out there? Something is worrying the dog". They said, "We have three friends with us, but we didn't want to scare you". I said, "Bring them in". They were hesitant, but finally entered. I don't think they were as much afraid of scaring me as wondering if my kitchen would hold them. What a group of huge men! We got talking of different things–one especially was sauerkraut.

One man said, "Oh my God–sauerkraut". I said, "Yes,

would you like to have some"? He fairly gasped "Yes", while the others asked what kind of stuff is that? They were all enjoying sauerkraut and bread, when Wentie and Dean came in. Wentie said, "I knew we had company". Wentie knew everything in advance. He was quite observant. He queried them about many things, especially the name and number of their ship. The boys were a bit leery of him and were evasive. Not so much at ease with him.

I gave the boys as much milk as I could spare, also a kettle of kraut and a piece of pork with directions for cooking. I asked them to bring my kettles back and they faithfully promised to comply.

Wentie continued keeping score of the comings and goings of the boats. Ten days went by, but no return of our boys. One of the boats had an obscure number and name due to camouflage. Wentie had talked about it. The boys had said, "It's our boat, the *Montreal*".

So the *Montreal* went out and did not return. With an amused smile, Wentie said to me, "You can say goodbye to your kettles. That's what you get for trusting everybody and their slick talk"! I didn't care too much as I was accustomed to friends being careless and not returning things. If my good deeds made a few sailors happy, we could credit it to the war effort.

Three days later I had the urge to do my weekend baking on Friday. Once again Wentie was out in the evening. About dusk six big men and a smaller one came to return my kettles, which were filled to overflowing with canteen goods–a rare treat for us.

Wentie arrived home. I had cookies and two squash pies. I just made two cuts in each pie, serving a quarter to each man. Those men were just like boys. One chap, a George Smith from Sault Ste. Marie, who had a Swedish wife, asked what kind of pie he was eating. I told him squash pie. He said, "I've never eaten squash pie that tasted this good before".

Bless those men, they were so gracious. They had come to

bid us goodbye. Wentie said, "I knew you weren't from the *Montreal*. You were too hesitant in answering me two weeks ago". They told him that they didn't want to get in trouble and had been protecting themselves.

We received mail from many mothers after the war ended for being so kind to their sons, while they were in His Majesty's service. Some of the boys who visited with us at the island told me that I reminded them of their mothers. One certain group came frequently, bringing a few different friends each time. The boys would call the lighthouse a home away from home.

One Sunday I had asked six boys to come for dinner. I cooked, but they didn't come. That evening they came. I asked "Why didn't you come for dinner"? They replied that it would make too much work for me.

I said, "I cooked kraut; will you have some now"? Some said yes; others said they did not know what it was, and one chap said, "I wouldn't eat that stuff, even for my own mother"! Wentie said, "Taste it". Well, he guessed he would try a little bit. After tasting it, he said, "I am ashamed of myself, but please, may I have another serving? I never saw nor tasted kraut like that before". Wentie said, "It's the way it was cooked."

Bert joined the air force in 1943. Dean left home about the same time. In a year or so there wasn't much traffic in the Bay. Things were very dull. Four of us on the island in our youth was far different living from two middle-aged adults with two very young children.

During the Second World War, civil servants were asked to subscribe a portion of their wages to the war cause. In addition, people were requested to buy war saving stamps at twenty-five cents each. When sixteen stamps were acquired, they were turned in to the government. At maturity the four dollars could be redeemed for five dollars.

Visitors to the island often gave the children small change. The children were encouraged to save their pennies for the war cause. One day we made up enough change for Wayne and Joyce to each buy a certificate. Wentie turned to me and said, "What will I put that 'chicken feed' in"? Joyce, hearing his question, left her chair in a mad dash and went to the feed shed. She quickly returned with a large sack to put the change in. She evidently hadn't heard that slang phrase before, but it sure gave her dad and me a good laugh.

For more years than I can remember, in our community people celebrated the old year out and the new year in by holding midnight services in the churches, ringing bells, holding parties, singing and dancing; but the greatest sport of men was to let out a volley of shots. I suspect the greatest joy in this was to determine whose gun created the loudest noise and to talk about the quality of the guns later (the best breach loader or granddad's old muzzle loader).

In 1944-45, on the hour of midnight, Wentie took out his old twelve-gauge shotgun. Someone on the mainland replied; the ships in the Bay took up the serenade and put on an array of splendor such as I had never witnessed before or since.

A lady living in Boutilier's Point, who was widely travelled, said that even in Paris she had not seen anything to equal the beauty of that night. I can only say that it was indescribable.

The boys onboard the ships knew it was a last fling for many of them and took advantage of the opportunity to go all out. We heard later that the "Big Brass" were dismayed at the misuse of so many military flares and rockets.

When Joyce was eight months old, she wasn't very well, so I wrote of her condition to the old doctor who had delivered her. By correspondence he diagnosed her condition as a liver ailment. He sent me a prescription, which we had filled. She was fine for almost a year. She would get sick for about two days, get better, but be listless and wan. Each six to eight weeks she would have a sick spell; the more frequent, the sicker she would be.

One night in March of 1940, it was raining and blowing quite a strong northeast gale. Joyce had been sick for several days. Wentie was quite withdrawn. Dean and I worriedly discussed Joyce's condition and decided that she should go to a doctor.

Bert came in from his customary stroll around the island. I said, "Bert, don't you think we should get Joyce to a doctor"? He said, "I think it's time somebody was doing something"! Wentie said, "I can't go (typical). I can't leave Wayne and Dean here alone. Bert, can you row your mother and Joyce ashore"? I couldn't believe my ears. However, he told Bert which course to row, helped us get into the big lighthouse boat with Joyce covered in canvas to give her protection from the storm.

Neither Bert nor I had wet weather clothes, but he was wearing a wind breaker. He said, "Don't be frightened, Mother, but I can't row in this thing". He pulled his oars before him and removed his jacket. It was raining so hard and he, poor kid, was only fifteen years old.

Finally, we landed in Boutilier's Point. He tied the boat, asked me if I could manage, took Joyce in his arms and carried her to Ethel's house. Harold was visiting Cliff Boutilier. Bert ran for him. Harold came and said he only had enough rationed gas to get him as far as Mason's store, but he was sure Mr. Mason would let him have enough gas to take a sick child to a doctor.

Bert was drenched to the skin as he started for home. Harold, Joyce and I left for Halifax. Mr. Mason, Heaven bless him, gave us the gas. We went to Dr. Carney, who had treated Wayne as an infant.

Dr. Carney went over Joyce, over and over again. He seemed puzzled, but said liver. I gasped. He said, "What"? Then I told him about her sickness when she was eight months old. He said, "Oh, that is it. She was born with insufficient liver". The work the liver had to do couldn't be done and the liver had to turn over periodically. The condition was diagnosed as cycling liver.

The cure was a white powder; DYNO, only thirty-five cents per package. It was similar to icing sugar, mildly sweet, and recommended for many uses including athletes. If it didn't control her condition by oral use, it would have to be administered by rectum. Thankfully, I never had to use the latter method, but we also had to have extra rations of sugar in her diet that could only be obtained with a doctor's prescription. The latter was grudgingly granted by the government after a wait of six months.

When we returned from Halifax, I was frozen and still very damp. Ethel and Harold slept on a couch in their kitchen, which I would have gladly accepted in preference for their bed. I was so-o-o c-c-cold.

Joyce got along quite well, but had to be careful with her diet and had to take a tonic. There was a possibility, if we could control the liver until she was twelve years old, we'd be lucky; otherwise she could develop asthma. She did not get asthma, but is subject to bronchitis and anemia.

Chapter eighteen

Oliver Dauphinee was a general merchant and postmaster at Boutilier's Point. He was a genial man, gracious to the public and delved into many types of businesses. He acquired property further inland and set up a sawmill, cookhouse and all. His store was located close to an excellent wharf, so he could use the sea for transportation. The railway also ran close by, so all in all he was in an ideal spot to do business.

Gradually, however, it became more feasible to use trucks to do his freighting. In this way he could go far inland and pick up large quantities of farm produce, including livestock. Ollie seldom went alone on these ventures. He usually took several men, or a man and his wife, or some members of his own family. The trips through beautiful Nova Scotia with a genial host such as Oliver were truly enjoyable. One day when Wentie was with him, he said, "Would Maggie ever enjoy a trip like this". Ollie said, "Well, we'll see that she gets a trip, and soon".

True to his word, the opportunity soon arrived, and Wentie and Ollie arranged for me to go. On the specified day the sun rose bright and beautiful, but I did not. I was subject to gall attacks and only those who have suffered from such an ailment can visualize the pain and nausea of this illness. I sure felt like someone had punched me in the tummy, and insisted on bringing their fist out my back. Wentie said, "You can't let Ollie down. Take a couple of aspirin and get dressed. I will take you in and if you still don't feel well then I'll bring you home".

I felt like a puppet being pulled on strings, but away we went. We were accompanied by Ollie's daughter, Jean, and his granddaughter, Eleanor. Ollie said, "I'm taking you up country with me, but first I'm taking you to a doctor in Halifax". That dear man went about twenty-five miles out of his way to take me to the doctor, who declared that the worst of the attack was over. He gave me a medication and said "You poor soul, go on your trip and enjoy it".

We were far behind schedule by this time. Ollie knew the nicest eating places and soon we stopped at a small place managed by a lady. I didn't want to eat, but Ollie said the nourishment would be good for me, and that we wouldn't get another opportunity for hours. I took some medication and, to my surprise, thoroughly enjoyed a delicious, well served meal.

We made another stop, where truck and car gadgets and tires were sold. One of the main reasons for this trip was to see if Ollie could find tires to fit his truck. The ones on which we rode were sadly in need of replacement. Ollie tried to buy tires, but they were not for sale. World War II had everything in short supply, so tires could only be bought with a government order.

We motored on to Kingsport. Ollie did some looking around in a garage there. The owners were really only getting set up for business. They were a young couple, recently married. The bride had started to crochet a tablecloth many years before and had laid the work aside until time permitted finishing it. In her new home she resumed crocheting, but her tension had so changed that she could not get the two pieces to match. I often wonder how much she accomplished in her second endeavour. By this time Ollie was ready to go again, still unsuccessful in his attempt to buy new tires for his truck.

Time was really fleeting and there was still much to be done, so we started out again. We went about a mile and a tenth, when I saw Ollie clench his jaw and throw himself, body and soul, across the steering wheel. The truck went hoppity, skippity, across the road. As it slowly lost speed, we watched as one of its wheels rolled down the road ahead of us. We finally came to a stop and climbed out. The girls went and rolled the wheel back. Ollie then told them to go back to the garage for the tow truck, in case he was unable to repair the wheel himself. While they were gone, Ollie jacked the truck up. The knowledge I had gained working with Wentie now came in handy. As Ollie lay on his back, working under the truck, I could hand him the tools that he needed, as I understood what he was asking for. We had just finished the job when Jean and Eleanor drove up with the garage man and his tow truck. We returned to the garage for confirmation that we could trust the truck. Ollie said that he was afraid to tighten the nuts too tightly for fear of stripping the threads on the bolts.

We retraced our tracks and headed for the strawberry fields, already three hours late. We picked more strawberries than I had ever seen before and bought many more crates of berries that had previously been picked.

Then we were off to a stockyard, where we looked over a carload of horses just arrived from sunny old Alberta. Ollie was not interested in buying any of these. We then moved on to a pen filled with wriggling young pigs and Ollie bought several litters.

The sun was dipping in the west, when Ollie thought of home. The roads weren't paved nor the speed so great in those days, so it was very dark when we stopped to have supper and limber up a bit. The drive home seemed endless. It was very dark along the country roads. Jean thought her father was looking tired and coaxed to be allowed to drive. The fact that she had only just received her license made Ollie a little reluctant to relinquish the wheel.

I think that we were coming into Waverly when fatigue got the better of caution, and Ollie traded seats with Jean. We were riding in a big old three or four-ton truck, and praying that the tires would hold, but Jean took to her chore like a duck to water, handling that big truck as though it was a car. Twas mere minutes before Ollie was breathing deeply and leaning wherever he could find support. Meanwhile, little Eleanor, who was about seven, had fallen asleep on my knee. We arrived at the Dauphinee home at 1:45 a.m., tired, but happy. It was a delightful experience for me as I did not often get away from the island for a mere pleasure trip. Usually, when our family was taken on a pleasure trip it meant hours of hard work, dreaming up a hearty lunch to enjoy by a brook or in a gravel pit by the roadside. We would exchange food with the party who took us out, hoping that our idea of a picnic lunch coincided with that of our hosts. My trip with Oliver, Jean and Eleanor spared me all this endeavour. It was truly a pleasant, enjoyable holiday.

The Dauphinees' hospitality did not end here. I was shown to a comfortable guest-room and told, with wishes I would rest well, not to get up until I felt fully awake. When I came into the pleasant kitchen the next morning, later than I care to admit, the table was set for one, coffee perked on the stove; bacon lay in a pan with eggs nearby. A note said, "Help yourself and meet us in the store at your leisure. Wentie picked me up later that day.

I returned home feeling better, both physically and mentally. I still can't believe that the trip took place so many years ago, because it is so vivid in my memory now.

Chapter nineteen

Wentie still was not well and declared that he could not work. One morning the left side of his head was swollen. He would not see a doctor. Through the Department of Veteran Affairs I found out that he had a disease of the head known as Paget's disease.

As for me, I was growing tired of life on the island and was going to leave one way or another. I asked Wentie to live a year among neighbors—give me a little of the freedom that I was so long denied. This he refused to do, so we moved to Indian Point with our nearest neighbour three-quarters of a mile away.

Wentie, the children and I landed there in a snowstorm at 4:00 p.m. on November 14, 1944, to be met by Mr. Will Dauphinee, 90 years old. We had a crate of a dozen or so hens, but it seemed to weigh a ton when Mr. Dauphinee put his cane aboard and hung on too. The house was desperately cold that night. We put two mattresses on the floor and all crawled in together. There was two feet of water in the cellar.

We still had to watch for good weather to get the remainder of our things from the island. What we couldn't get within a few weeks was stolen—some furniture, fishing gear and Wentie's tools. Locks proved to be no barrier to vandals and thieves. In a few years the buildings were razed, yet even the R.C.M.P. couldn't catch up with the villains.

The government, by letter, asked Wentie and me to keep an eye on the lighthouse for a small compensation. We did so. One day we saw a group there, so Wentie and I went over. It was a group of young lads from Black Point. They gave us a song and dance story of having just arrived and knew nothing of the damage that had taken place. Wentie did not turn them in.

Another day he saw people there. We phoned the report to the Department of Transport and Supply. Two days later the R.C.M.P. drove into our yard at Indian Point wanting to know what had happened. We didn't get any recognition for our efforts, so no longer watched on behalf of the government.

We didn't know how to make money farming any better than we did fishing. Wentie's Civil Service pension was very low and, of course, I was not compensated for my work. To save money we cut enough logs on Indian Point, to saw lumber for a house and barn in Tantallon. When we were ready to build, we had to buy lumber as ours had been stolen.

In 1942 I was operated on for gall stones. Grace and I were both in the Halifax Infirmary at the same time. She had one big stone and felt fine after her operation. I didn't have any stones, but an inflamed bladder that was buried so deeply in the liver that they were unable to remove it.

In December, 1948, while living on Indian Point, I was badly troubled. I went to the Ladies Aid in the afternoon. That evening I wanted to finish painting an oilcloth design on the pantry floor. I worked long into the night and thought, "I'm so tired, but I must finish it because there is so much to do before Christmas". I went to bed around 3:00 p.m. I was deathly sick for two days. We finally got a Dr. Braine from Seabright. He didn't think I was very sick. He said I'd be good as new in a few days, but I was sicker than ever.

Bert was home on leave from the R.C.M.P. Dean was called home from Rockingham, where she was employed. They called in a doctor from Hubbards. He ordered me to a hospital. Bert and Wentie helped me downstairs to the car, where I practically fell into the back seat, and I remembered nothing else for almost a week.

On December 13 I was operated on again for gallstones. There were hundreds of them there, so embedded in the liver that the doctor felt that he had cut too deep, but it was a risk that he had to take. Since then I have had to be extremely careful of my diet, having uncomfortable times, but telling folks that I'm awfully well for the shape I'm in!

I did eventually get back to the farm, took in boarders, went out housecleaning and baked to help supplement our small pension; meanwhile, Wentie earned a little here and a bit there.

Wayne had gone to work for Eaton's, but came home for the winter to study and help his dad—neither proved successful. Wayne returned to Halifax, where he hired on with a hardware store, until, in 1952, he was old enough to join the R.C.M.P.

We boarded Joyce with her sister, Dean(who had married Oliver Stevens), and later she stayed with Ethel so that she could attend a vocational school in Halifax. We moved into our new home in Tantallon on January 11, 1955, and she then returned home.

One day a veteran of World War II was here on insurance business. He asked me what was wrong with Wentie. I said, "I don't know—he has complained all his life". The insurance man said, "He is sick. Does he get a pension"? I said, "No". He replied, "What a pity". We talked some. Wentie never did get a pension until illness placed him in Camp Hill Hospital. He had been in several times for treatment and was placed there permanently in September, 1969. He died there on August 28, 1972.

During one terrible storm, while we were at Indian Point, things were very destructive. A boatbuilder in Seabright had just finished building a boat and had it at anchor only a few days. It broke adrift as the storm raged all night. Wentie saw it leave its mooring at dusk. Everybody was sure that the boat was doomed.

Next morning the sun shone beautifully, as so often happens after the fury of a storm. A group of men came to see the pieces of his boat, where it landed on the Nubic and now lay.

Not more than a few scratches showed on the paint. Otherwise, it could have been stored in a boathouse. That was a miracle of miracles; how that boat rode the waves over the reef of rocks. This man was a pious, good-living man. The care of his boat was one of God's mercies.

I don't think there was anything spectacular in our lives. Was it a challenge? Many have lived in isolation. Many have stood by helplessly watching their loved ones die without medical aid, strengthened only by the presence of others as helpless as the bereaved one.

I remember one of my mother's stories of childhood days. She would tell how her mother kept clothes in the barn. When Gran'ma or Aunt Ellen was sent for, she went to the barn, changed her clothes before going to a friend's house, where there was sickness. When returning home, she once again went to the stable and changed her clothes to protect her own children against diphtheria and small pox, the two most dreaded diseases in the days of the pioneers. It was not unusual to take a child to the cemetery, return home and find another child dead. She mentioned the above happened to Mr. and Mrs. George Smith.

Mother's cousin, Ada, had ten children and saved only one boy and one girl to grow to adulthood. Our good friend, a fisherman of Boutilier's Point, told us that when the plague was at its peak, a Mr. and Mrs. Boutilier had lost so many of their seventeen children that it was soul searing.

One morning Mr. Boutilier went to the cooper shop to get a pine board to make a little coffin. He didn't have enough pine. As he opened the shop door to go look for some pine boards, his wife stood in the house doorway calling "Make two, there is another gone". He went back, further inland and met a Mr. Garrison. The latter said, "What's wrong? You seem fretful. Have you lost another child"? "Yes, two. I'm looking for a board to make another coffin".

Mr. Garrison said, "This won't do! I am confirmed, which gives me the right to perform the burial rites. You go exhume those other little bodies that are buried on the farm, and bring them all over to the consecrated grounds. We will give them all a righteous burial.

I have not seen the little headstone, which marks their place of burial in St. James Anglican Church Cemetery in Boutilier's Point, but several of the old people, most of whom are now deceased, told me the same story.

When I think of some of the stories the men told of their youth, some experiences told to me by my mother-in-law, and others of which I have read, I've reason to believe that my life as a lightkeeper's wife on Croucher's Island was well lived. We were surrounded by beauty with no difficulty too great to surmount, with a Supreme Being watching over us at all times.

Epilogue

Upon leaving Croucher's Island in November, 1944, the author, her husband and two youngest children took up residence on Indian Point in Glen Haven. She lived there for ten years and during this time her son left home. She continued a lifestyle that was similar to life on the island: farming, gardening, sewing, knitting, crocheting, tatting, mat hooking, quilting, baking, and cooking (this included making butter and curd, puddings, sausage and potted head, jams, jellies, pickles and chows). She took in vacationers during the summers and cared for her husband's ailing sister during the last four years there.

Her main feat on Indian Point was getting electricity installed in our house. Her first trip to town found her standing before a board of men—just where this took place is unknown. However, she was refused as she was over a half mile away from the nearest light pole. Since a member of the board had a summer cottage a mile away from her, it annoyed her to think that he had such good lighting. Someone discovered the nearest summer cottage was just a half mile away from her, and they had lights, so she returned to again face the board. Within a year, believed to be the fall of 1946, she had electric lights.

In January, 1954, they moved to Tantallon from where she visited Western, Eastern and Upper Canadian relatives, as well as some in the United States. She made other trips throughout Canada and the United States trying to improve her vision, which started to deteriorate after surgery in 1946, but was unsuccessful.

She wrote this book between 1981 and 1985. Getting it published was almost impossible until the spring of 2002. Actual work started in 2003.

On June 29, 1986, she took ill and entered hospital on July 4, where "a little touch of infection" (diagnosed in emergency at another hospital on June 29) started her downward battle for life. She died late in the day of August 8. June 29 is her youngest son's birthday and August 8 is the day before her youngest daughter's birthday.

Joyce Cook
June 19, 2003